TRUE ADVENTURES

THE BLACK PIMPERNEL

NELSON MANDELA ON THE RUN

ZUKISWA WANNER
With illustrations by Amerigo Pinelli

PUSHKIN CHILDREN'S

Pushkin Press
71–75 Shelton Street
London WC2H 9JQ

Text © Zukiswa Wanner 2021
Illustrations © Amerigo Pinelli 2021

First published by Pushkin Press in 2021

1 3 5 7 9 8 6 4 2

ISBN 13: 978-1-78269-307-9

Designed and typeset by Tetragon, London
Printed and bound by CPI Group (UK) Ltd, Croydon, CR0 4YY

www.pushkinpress.com

THE BLACK PIMPERNEL

NOTE: PLACE NAMES ARE GIVEN AS THEY WERE AT THE TIME
TANGANYIKA IS NOW TANZANIA, AND BECHUANALAND IS NOW BOTSWAN

PROLOGUE

THE END OF DAVID

5 AUGUST, 1962

'Are you ready, David?' his travelling companion asks.

'Yes I am, Mister Williams,' the man called David says.

It is their little inside joke whenever they travel together and are not in safe spaces.

Sometimes David even calls him *baas*, the Afrikaans word that white men expect to hear from black or brown men. A word that means 'master' and shows that they are in charge. That they are the 'boss'.

Cecil Williams is older than David.

In the hierarchy of the anti-apartheid movement that they both belong to, however, David would be the boss.

But David is black and Cecil is white.

In South Africa of 1962, a country where a man is judged by his race, the black man is always expected to serve the white man. This policy of racial segregation, the law in South Africa, is known as *apartheid*.

David makes sure he carries himself like the respectful chauffeur he is supposed to be. He carries Cecil's briefcase and puts it on the back seat. 'Will you sit at the back with your briefcase, Mister Williams, sir?' he asks as he opens the back door and doffs his cap.

Cecil, a theatre director who rather enjoys performing as much as he enjoys directing performance, answers, 'No, old chap. You know what? I think I will drive today since you drove on your way here. I have a lot of work for you when we return to Johannesburg, so you will drive enough.'

David lowers his hat, opens the door for Cecil, and when Cecil is seated, he goes round and sits on the front passenger seat. He feels his revolver, a gift from his military trainer in Ethiopia, in its holster inside his jacket.

Once they start driving, they both relax.

'You must be tired, comrade,' Cecil says.

'Exhausted. The trip and everything I did had to be done but I cannot wait to sleep for a few days.' Then David's eyes light up. 'And of course there is Winnie. My poor wife. Widowed while I am alive. It will be so good to see her and the children.'

Cecil grunts in agreement but says nothing, leaving David alone with his thoughts.

Today, they are driving in the light of day.

David prefers it that way.

Night brings cover, but there is also the unknown. In their hunt for him, the police seem to imagine that he travels only at night and that is when they set roadblocks.

Two days ago when he arrived in Bechuanaland, the magistrate told him the South African police were already on the lookout for him.

Did someone in the movement let slip that he is coming back?

David shakes his head from the negative thought and looks outside. The route from Durban to Johannesburg is one of the most beautiful parts of his country. The hills and valleys are brown with some sparse greenery. The South African winter has just ended, but in this part of the country the weather is always warm and welcoming. He wonders if the hills have any caves.

He chuckles to himself. He has really started thinking more like a soldier than a politician.

'What?' Cecil asks, taking his eyes from the road for a moment and looking at him.

'Nothing,' David says.

He is thinking of his soldiers, well-trained and well-armed, using the caves up these hills as bases. They would be able to do some covert operations in Durban, Pietermaritzburg and surrounding areas from there without being detected, he thinks. And should someone finally find out where they are, assuming they come and investigate without helicopters first, they could hurl some boulders down the hills and cause some damage while escaping.

He looks outside again, this time as the man who grew up in the village but has become a city man.

He remembers the freedom of the outside.

He never tires of the beauty that he sees when he travels this road.

And today as he is travelling, as tired as he is, he is feeling happy even as he worries about the police. He is happy because he managed to brief the leaders of his organization, the African National Congress (ANC), on his travels on the continent and beyond.

Travels which were as fruitful to the movement as they were to him as the commander-in-chief of the armed wing of the movement, *uMkhonto we Sizwe*, Spear of the Nation. He believes that the training he received while he was away will allow him to truly be the spear that pricks the nation's conscience. He hopes that perhaps through their military tactics, the President of South Africa, Hendrik Verwoerd, and his government can begin to see all people as equal whether black, white or brown.

Not everyone agrees but the man in the passenger seat believes that only an armed revolution will free them from the yoke of the apartheid state.

As far as the apartheid government is concerned, South Africa belongs to the Europeans and everyone else is there to serve them in different degrees.

The Asians have fewer privileges than the Europeans.

The Coloureds – a mixture of either Asian and African or African and European who failed to pass for whites, or Africans who succeeded in passing for Coloured perhaps with their softer curls that a pencil could fall through and lighter complexions – have it better than the Africans.

And then there are the Africans. In the opinion of the Europeans, and sometimes everyone else in this country without African origin, they are at the bottom.

Not on his watch, David thinks again with a sense of euphoria. Not any more. As commander-in-chief of *uMkhonto we Sizwe*, he plans to change this.

'This land is beautiful,' he says to his companion who is driving. 'No wonder they will do anything to keep it, including inventing lies that there was no one living here when they first arrived.'

He is happy too that on his trip he met with the Durban Command led by Bruno Mtolo.

It was the first time he had met Bruno but he had heard good things about him. There had been one or two complaints about his drinking, but from what David saw of him yesterday, it is nothing to worry about.

Bruno has briefed him about the base they have set up in Durban's Kloof neighbourhood.

A neighbourhood meant for Europeans on African soil.

Bruno justifies being there by pretending to be a gardener to one of their white comrades.

The irony.

Perhaps this is what it means to be 'servant leaders'.

The Durban Command has been doing well with their acts of sabotage. David laughed with them and complimented them on blowing up a power station that caused darkness for a while in the city of Durban earlier in the year.

He is happy too because, after briefing both the party and the Durban Command, the comrades in Durban hosted a party for him. They called it a 'welcome home' party as he had just arrived back into the country. They also called it a 'farewell party' as he was leaving Durban to return to Johannesburg.

He looks in the rear-view mirror as he remembers the music and dancing and he gets anxious. 'Cecil,' he says to the man who is driving.

Cecil hears the seriousness in his voice, takes his eyes off the road briefly again and answers, 'Yes, David?'

They both laugh a little. The use of this name, David, continues to be a source of amusement to them both. In the safety of the car, they can laugh.

'You know this lawless state machinery wants me,' David says, warming up to his subject. 'How many years do you think they would give me if they knew that I'm now not just a speaker but am also a guerrilla, military-trained?'

Cecil does a small whistle before answering, 'You are a lawyer, so what do your law books say? A life sentence?'

He shakes his head and replies, 'It won't be a life sentence. They want me dead. Definitely the death sentence.'

David's anxiety increases. He is a father of five; if anything were to happen to him, what would happen to his children?

He smiles a little nervously but then remembers that he has nothing to worry about. He has good comrades across the racial groups. They would be loyal to his memory and look after his family.

Then he shakes his head.

Lately his feelings of apprehension have almost always become equal to his feelings of joy.

'Nothing will happen to me,' he whispers under his breath to give himself courage.

The apartheid police fumble, and for the last year and a half his greatest strength has been hiding in plain sight.

'Do you think my little Zindzi will remember me? I have been away for so long,' he asks Cecil.

'It may take a couple of days before she does but eventually she will,' Cecil answers earnestly. 'In fact,' he adds, 'that beard of yours may throw her off. Maybe even scare her for a while.'

David caresses his chin with his right hand, feeling his beard. Should he shave off the beard? he wonders briefly. But he has become used to it and he likes it. The apartheid police are looking for a clean-shaven man. If he shaves his beard, he is setting himself up to get caught.

'Ja. Nee?' he says, rubbing his face again. 'I guess her tata will have to scare his little girl for a while. I have soldiers to recruit and train for the revolution.'

But then his unease returns.

'Did you see that Ford V-8?' he asks as soon as they leave the small town of Howick, twenty miles out of Pietermaritzburg. They have been on the road for a little over an hour.

'I saw it. It's been following us from Pietermaritzburg,' Cecil answers. 'Oh, wait. Maybe we are both just overly worried,' he says as the car goes past them.

It is full of white men.

'Or maybe not. There are two more of its kind behind us,' David says, while hiding his notebook and a revolver in the space between the two front seats.

The car that passed them signals them to stop.

As Cecil slows down and parks, he asks, 'Who are these men?'

He knows who the men are. They both do.

The man Cecil referred to as David wishes he could jump out of the car and make a dash for it.

But that would be foolish. There is nowhere to run and these men will have no qualms about shooting him in the back.

He sits still and can only hope that the gun and the notebook will not be found. If they are, it's a death sentence for him.

A man walks over from the parked car. He is looking haggard, as though he has been awake for days. He walks directly to the passenger side and asks the passenger to open his window.

Then he introduces himself. 'My name is Sergeant Vorster of the South African Police, what is your name?'

'I am David Motsamayi,' the passenger answers.

'Where are you coming from and where are you going?'

'I had driven my baas,' he says, nodding to the driver, 'to Durban for some business.'

'And why is your baas driving now?'

'My baas, he is a good baas, baas. He said I should rest a little bit and I can continue driving from Harrismith,' he answers.

'You think this is a joke?' Sergeant Vorster says, sounding irritated. 'I am here to arrest you. I know who you are,' he adds, producing a warrant of arrest.

The passenger looks at it. 'My name is David Motsamayi. This,' he says, pointing at the arrest warrant, 'this is not my name, baas.'

Sergeant Vorster has had enough. He points his gun at the passenger. 'Get out. Get out of that car now.'

The passenger obliges but feels the need to add, 'But baas, I am not—'

'Shut up. I know who you are. You are Nelson Mandela and that is Cecil Williams, and you are both under arrest.'

Nelson realizes that the game is up. He puts his hands behind his back.

He's been seventeen months underground, and in some way he feels relieved.

He does not have to hide any more.

He can now be himself.

He can now shave the beard.

When the Durban comrades called the party yesterday a 'farewell party', did any of them know?

MARCH 1961

❖❖❖

JOHANNESBURG, SOUTH AFRICA

Seventeen months earlier

1

The time comes in the life of any nation when there remains only two choices: **submit or fight!**

THAT TIME has now come to **South Africa!**

A SERVANT OF THE MOVEMENT

24th March, 1961

It is late morning in a house in Johannesburg. It's in this Parktown suburb that twelve members of the National Working Committee, along with a few supporters, shall gather. Two African women in domestic workers' uniforms have just got off the bus. They walk together and ring the bell at a gate of a house. The house has a high and solid white gate. It opens and they enter.

Twenty-six minutes later, a small pick-up truck driven by an Indian man arrives at the same address. Once inside the gate, eight people – six African men, two Indian women, the driver and another Indian man who was on the passenger seat emerge from the vehicle.

One of the men would be called a Coloured in this country because of his fair skin. Everyone refers to him as an African. He identifies himself as an African, thereby ignoring what privileges he may be able to get because of the shade of his skin. Walter Sisulu is wearing a casual shirt and trousers. Among the men to emerge, he is the shortest.

Two of the African men are wearing suits and have short hair with side partings as is the fashion of the day for gentlemen of their standing. One of them is tall with a bulky frame, befitting the boxing exercises he undertakes when he can spare a few minutes from fighting against apartheid.

Professionally, they are legal partners, Nelson Mandela and Oliver Tambo. Oliver is shorter than Nelson, but a lot of people are shorter than Nelson.

In this gathering, Oliver and Nelson are respectively Secretary-General of the African National Congress (ANC) and chief organizer for the Boycott Campaign.

The two women in domestic workers' uniforms, and five other people – three men and two women, all European – emerge from the house to greet everyone else.

Oliver does not allow the chit-chat to happen for long.

'Let's go inside, comrades. We never know who is watching. Let's talk about what needs to be done so we can leave before anyone gets suspicious and raids this house.'

He walks in and the others follow. The house belongs to Ruth First and her husband, Joe Slovo, a white couple and members of this committee, but Oliver walks in as though he is in familiar territory.

He is.

This is one of the homes that they have secret meetings in.

It is easier for the African, Coloured and Indian members of the movement to come to the white areas without raising eyebrows than it is for the Europeans to go to the townships where the Africans stay. There, the Europeans would stick out like sore thumbs.

But in the European areas, Africans and Coloureds could be domestic workers to the Europeans. The Indians, believed to be the merchant class in this country, could be coming to sell vegetables in their pick-up trucks to their European clients.

They all find seats and try to fit around a table that normally sits eight people. It does not take long for everyone to settle down and Oliver, who is chairing the meeting, starts to speak.

'The apartheid state continuously bans all of us in the leadership of the movement,' he begins.

The other members around respond, 'Eh he.' An affirmation of his statement, and an encouragement to continue.

'We can no longer go on as if it's business as usual.'

To strong murmurs of, 'Yes, yes.'

'It is now business *un*usual, and we must realize that the apartheid government will not relent but will only make things tougher.'

Chants of, 'Yes, Chair.'

'Verwoerd showed us his hand and declared war on us when he was still Minister of Native Affairs, and now that he is Prime Minister, he has tightened the noose on our freedoms.'

Oliver pauses like the good orator that he is, to take in the nods.

'Verwoerd and his cronies took it upon themselves to have a referendum in which only the minority could vote, and they have decided to declare this nation – our nation – a republic without even speaking to us.'

He pauses to take a sip of water, then continues.

'Comrades, to them anyone not of the same skin colour as themselves does not matter. This is what a declaration of a republic with only whites allowed to vote means. It also means we are in a state of war and we must fight against the powerful, armed regime of Verwoerd in every way possible.'

He pauses to let his words sink in.

'But as the massacre of sixty-nine people in Sharpeville showed us, as the massacres in Langa showed us, the enemy does not fight fairly and we must change our tactics.'

The atmosphere is electric. If a pin dropped on the carpeted floor, one could hear it.

'Let's learn from our brothers and sisters in Cuba who successfully overthrew the elite ruling class of Batista.'

'Yes, Chair.'

'Is there anyone among you who has objections to us now going underground and implementing the M-Plan?'

One of the women raises her hand. 'Who must go underground, Chair?'

'Some of us,' Oliver answers.

A man wants clarity. 'Erm, Chair. What does it mean – going underground?'

Oliver sighs. Was this man not listening when they discussed this before? With exaggerated patience, he says, 'It means that those of us with certain roles in the near future must avoid being visible wherever possible. Where we can, we stay with the least suspicious of our comrades in whatever role will make us invisible. Are there any objections?'

Murmurs of, 'no objection', and, 'it's about time'.

Oliver reminds them again how the M-Plan works.

'Communication will be on a need-to-know basis. The leaders in the sub-branches communicate individually to their local branch, the head of the branch to the district, the district to the region until the information gets to the top. Information will filter down to the branches in a similar manner. It might seem like a slower system than calling for a meeting of all movement supporters, but it is a safer system. This way, should anyone be caught, they can only betray the person who is their immediate senior, without betraying the whole system.'

As he finishes speaking, Oliver rests his chin on his forefingers, looks at everyone around the table slowly, and then rests his eyes on Nelson. In here, Nelson is not his legal partner. He is his comrade but also his subordinate in the leadership ranking.

And yet, he is also the single most important man in this room. More important than Oliver, even in terms of the direction of their movement.

Nelson has been tasked with mobilizing members of the movement and their supporters across the country in boycotts as a protest against the declaration of the republic. Nelson sits up straight when Oliver looks at him.

Then Oliver's eyes sweep the rest of the room. 'Our movement is officially going underground, and Nelson' – he turns his attention to his legal partner – 'as architect of the M-Plan, we expect you to go underground with it.'

Nelson Rolihlahla Mandela hesitates. 'Is it perhaps not better for me to go underground after the court case?'

The government accused a lot of people of treason nearly five years ago now, using a law against Communism, and Nelson is one of those who has to appear in court for the final verdicts next week.

'No, Nelson,' Oliver responds. 'We are not suggesting that you not turn up for the final court hearing, because we know you are a man of honour. What we are suggesting rather is that you practise to be underground immediately. We expect you in Maritzburg for the Congress conference though. You shall deliver a keynote speech but you are to arrive there as a surprise.'

Nelson is conflicted, but he smiles. The movement is his first family. 'I am a servant of the movement,' he says humbly. 'Whatever you decide, Secretary-General, I shall do.'

Oliver sums up the meeting. 'The movement is now officially underground and with it, our chief campaigner, Nelson Mandela. Many of us will have to try and act as normally as possible so that we can distract the apartheid police. If we all act like we are underground, nothing will be fruitful. Comrades, meeting adjourned.'

As they have some tea, Nelson and his comrades converse some more and pore over the speech he'll make at the conference.

When he leaves the meeting an hour later, foremost on his mind is how he will explain to his twenty-five-year-old wife, Winnie, that he is about to go underground. And yet he is also not too worried. She is not just his wife. She is also his comrade. A few years ago, a little while after their marriage, she had surprised him by joining older women in the movement in protesting against pass laws and getting imprisoned. His law firm with Oliver had represented them.

When Nelson enters the house, it's as though Winnie has had a forewarning of this. All she asks him is, 'How long will you be gone?'

'I don't know, s'thandwa sam',' he says, affectionately stroking her arm. She smiles warmly when he says that. *S'thandwa sam'*. My love. Not 'Mama Zenani' as other husbands would say: as though she lost her identity as his love when she had a child. No. *His love*.

He continues, 'I *really* don't know. But if you need anything, please talk to Albertina and Walter. Helen and Lillian will also contact you every now and again to check up on you.'

'Nelson, you realize the only person that could prove useful to me there is Walter's wife, Albertina? We don't know what will happen when they finalize the trial next week. You, Helen, Lillian and Walter may all end up in prison.' Winnie laughs a mirthless laugh.

'Don't say that, even as a joke, darling,' he admonishes playfully.

She nods her head, smiles and decides to deflect from the impending ruling. 'Why don't you go across into Orlando East to say goodbye to the older children while I am packing for you?'

Winnie may understand the politics that lead Nelson to his actions but he is embarrassed that he is leaving her at such a time, when their two daughters together are both under three. Yet he would rather leave them now to fight so that they can live in a South Africa that will treat them with dignity, than have them treated like second-class citizens in their own land.

He responds awkwardly, 'I was thinking the same thing.'

His oldest child – from his first marriage – is in Umtata, but he picks up his son, Makgatho, and daughter, Makaziwe, his other two children from that marriage. He drives them to their favourite veld, parks the car and they all get out to walk. It's a walk the three of them have taken often and that they enjoy. If they wait until after sunset, as they sometimes do, they will be able to see the lights of Johannesburg. Today though, they will not. He has a journey he needs to undertake.

'How long will you be gone, tata?' Makgatho asks earnestly.

'I don't know, my boy. But I want you to listen to your mother and take care of your sister,' Nelson replies.

'I can take care of myself, tata,' his seven-year-old daughter Makaziwe asserts fiercely. 'Maybe you should be asking me to take care of Makgatho instead.'

Nelson laughs, and inside as he looks at them, he strengthens his resolve again. His children, *all* children, are too beautiful to grow up in an abnormal society like this one. He doesn't know whether he will ever be able to secure their freedom but he will die fighting to do so. They talk some more and laugh, then race to the car. He holds his pace back and winks at Makgatho to do the same.

'I won. I beat you both like we will beat the whites, tata,' Makaziwe says.

Nelson smiles at the analogy.

When he gets home, his travelling companion, another African man, has arrived. If they are stopped by police, they have decided they will tell the police that they are going to a wedding.

They must get going.

Nelson kisses his wife and his two youngest children.

Winnie, who is holding the girls in her arms, blinks back tears and smiles.

'*Hamba kahle,*' she whispers. Go well.

Zenani, the older of the two girls, starts crying. Seeing her older sister crying, the younger Zindziswa joins in.

Winnie admonishes the girls and whispers to Zenani that she will not give her chocolate. The tears stop as fast they had begun.

With the children no longer crying, Nelson separates from his family and gets in the car.

He wonders when he will ever be able to be a normal parent to his children and a husband to his wife. Whether he will ever be so again.

As he starts the car, he looks at them one last time.

He shall be back for the verdict in the Treason Trial, of which he is one of the remaining accused. But with this separation from his family, his underground life has begun.

2

AN ANTI-REPUBLIC CONFERENCE

The police already know about the conference at Arya Samaj Hall in Pietermaritzburg.

In order for it to proceed, the organizers needed to get clearance from them.

Fifty policemen are inside the hall. They all have their radios in case of any hint of trouble.

More men are outside.

And others are on standby in Pietermaritzburg, Durban and nearby small towns like Howick.

Warrant Officer Truter, who is one of the witnesses at the Treason Trial, is one of those in the hall. He is in charge of the police on the right-hand side of the hall.

There is also Sergeant Vorster and an African detective, Sergeant Maxwell Levy Marwa.

Despite being of a lower rank than Truter, Vorster has been placed in charge of this operation. Rumours say he is related to the Minister of Justice, B.J. Vorster. The Sergeant denies it but Truter believes it. There is no other explanation why someone with a lower rank would have been put in charge of the operation.

Vorster and Marwa are next to each other on the left-hand side. The job of the policemen inside is to make these singing natives understand state power. That they can gather here only because the South African government of Verwoerd allows them to.

'So you see, Max,' Vorster continues their chat, 'the government is not unreasonable. Anywhere else, people who speak against the government would not have been able to get a permit to have such a conference. They would have been arrested. The native in this country does not know how lucky he is.'

Marwa nods his head vigorously but wonders, not for the first time, whether all these Europeans really believe everything they say.

Does Vorster believe that he, Maxwell Levy Marwa, is happier with lesser pay for the same rank?

Does he believe that he, Maxwell Levy Marwa, does not want his children attending less crowded schools? That his wife also would not want a maid to cook and clean up after the family?

But Marwa is a practical man. He joined the police *force* – it is definitely not a service – because he is the eldest in his family and he has to put his brothers and a sister through school. He hopes they can attain enough of an education to avoid the police force. Maybe one of them will get a degree from a university. He smiles privately to himself as he thinks this.

There is a lot of singing going on.

It is a large crowd.

The 1,500-strong crowd are singing songs of freedom.

Among them is the classic struggle song by Vuyisile Mini, *Ndod'emnyama*: Black Man.

> *Nants'indoda emnyama Verwoerd*
> *Nants'indoda emnyama Verwoerd*
> *Pasopa nants'indoda emnyama Verwoerd*
> *Pasopa nants'indoda emnyama Verwoerd*

'What are they saying, Max? I can hear them saying the Prime Minister's name,' Vorster says.

'It's nothing much. When they mention the Prime Minister's name, they are thanking him for allowing them to gather,' Marwa says, trying to keep a straight face.

He knows Vorster would call for back-up and close this meeting if he knew what all these people are actually singing:

Here comes the black man, Verwoerd.
Beware, here comes the black man, Verwoerd.

It's a catchy tune.

Marwa wishes he could join in.

Instead he just hums under his breath.

Soon enough, a man walks onto the stage.

There is a collective gasp and for a few seconds everyone in the hall is quiet.

Even the police did not expect this man.

'Is that…?' Vorster asks.

'That is…' Marwa says at the same time.

'It's Nelson Mandela,' they say in unison.

'Did you know?' Vorster asks Marwa.

Marwa shrugs his shoulders. He had no idea. This appears to have been a strongly guarded secret.

Suddenly the crowd starts singing their song again with more energy than before.

Marwa is convinced that at this time, if he gave each of these people a gun, they would liberate themselves and him. The energy is palpable.

The black man who Verwoerd should be afraid of dances a little on stage as he sings along.

The song is repeated a few times.

Vorster and Truter look across at each other and one signals to the other that their men – black plainclothes policemen – are already in different spaces in the crowd.

The Master of Ceremony quiets the crowd. He pumps his fist up and passionately chants the slogan, 'Amandla.'

Marwa translates before Vorster asks. *Amandla*. Power. They respond, '*Awethu*.' Is ours.

He repeats it and they answer back with just as much strength.

Vorster and Truter look at each other in panic. They don't know this chant that the natives always seem to start their meetings with, but if they were to turn on them, they are outnumbered.

The emcee greets them, 'Sawubona.' He is in Natal with a largely Zulu-speaking population. It is fitting that he starts with their language.

The crowd replies, 'Yebo.'

'Dumelang,' he greets them in Sesotho.

'A-ge,' they respond.

'Molweni,' he greets again in isiXhosa.

'Molo,' they reply.

'My fellow South Africans. I greet you all in the name of Congress,' he continues, and then he quickly remembers that the African National Congress is now a banned entity, so he self-corrects, 'that is, I greet you all in the name of freedom.'

Marwa takes out his pen and notebook and starts writing. He really wants to hear what the great Nelson Mandela has to say, but he has to pretend he is taking the notes as part of his job.

'Before we start our proceedings, please can you stand so that we sing our anthem?' the emcee requests.

Everyone stands and starts singing the African anthem that has become the song of freedom for many independent parties in this part of the African continent: *Nkosi Sikelel' iAfrika*. The crowd sings the verses in isiZulu. In isiXhosa. In Sesotho. *Lord bless Africa, let it be exalted. Hear our prayers. We, the African family.* Then the call for the spirit to come down and the request that this God of Africa makes it happen.

To Marwa and many of the Africans listening, it is more than a song. It is a prayer. A rallying call.

Vorster, on the other hand, is wondering something different. He wonders why the natives have such a resistance to Afrikaans. They obviously have a propensity for languages. That anthem of theirs has more than one language, yet despite their different tribal languages, they know all the words. Why don't they care to speak the beautiful language of their rulers since they have no problem speaking the language of Kitchener, who killed a lot of people in concentration camps during the Anglo-Boer War?

That's why the natives should never be allowed the majority vote.

Fools, the lot of them.

Always being led badly by the Communists.

Like this Mandela who has just come on stage.

And as he thinks that, Nelson – who is the keynote speaker – starts talking.

He begins by chanting the slogan and the excited audience responds.

Nelson calls for a national convention in which South Africans of all racial groups create a constitution that mirrors the dreams of the country. In his speech, he states his belief that if all racial groups worked together for a common good and towards a common humanity, South Africa would be invincible.

His speech is in response to the all-white referendum that occurred in October 1960 to declare South Africa a republic but without any input from other racial groups. He calls upon all those assembled to reject the white Republic – agreed by the National Party, the majority party of a white minority – which will be declared on the 31st of May.

'If we do not act,' he says, while looking directly at the note-taking Sergeant Marwa, who looks down in embarrassment but continues writing, 'we will betray the people of Pondoland, Zeerust and Sekhukhuneland. Our course is to fight shoulder to shoulder for that great idea – the liberation of all the oppressed people in South Africa,' he finishes, to a standing ovation from the audience.

Vorster has directed people to follow him, but there is a crowd moving with Nelson. None of the police seem to notice where he has disappeared to. The police stay around for the final day of the conference but they do not see Nelson again.

Could he have gone back to Johannesburg? Vorster wonders.

He and his team shall continue to wonder.

What they do not know, what they will know only later on, is that Nelson Mandela stays at the conference, well-hidden until after the final day.

A SHORT END TO A LONG TRIAL

On the morning of the 29th of March, it seems as though all the movement's supporters and all members of the police are gathered at the Old Synagogue.

Some of the defendants have arrived and stand by themselves.

The police have deliberately decided to use themselves to create a space between the defendants and their hordes of supporters. Sergeant Vorster and Warrant Officer Truter are among the police that are there.

It is a clear show of force and power.

The defendants are talking to each other nervously. They have no idea what will happen at the end of this morning. Will they be getting prison sentences or can they expect to go home to their families?

Among those standing are Walter Sisulu and Joe Slovo, who are chatting animatedly with each other. Joe's wife Ruth, though not one of the defendants, has begrudgingly been allowed to stand with them after she showed the police her press card. She and Joe hold each other and he constantly rubs her shoulders as though to reassure her, even though he does not know what the verdict will be.

Every time Walter looks up to the crowd of supporters, he gives them the movement's thumbs-up signal and smiles. To their supporters, Walter's smile is reassuring. It says, we will get through this.

To the police, Walter's smile and his signal is cheeky. What makes this man smile when he may end up in prison by the end of today? Or is he smiling out of nervousness?

A Jaguar Mark 2 arrives near the entrance and the driver beeps so that people can get out of the way. The police and the crowd part as its driver parks as close to the entrance as possible.

Nelson emerges from the driver's side. Shouts can be heard from the crowd: 'It's Mandela!' And, 'Big man.'

Whoever yelled 'big man' does not know that a bigger man is about to appear.

Mandela opens the back door of the car and there he is: Israel 'Issy' Maisels, who is leading the defence team. He is as big in physical size as he is in his reputation as a good lawyer. Walter's wife, Albertina, also comes out from the back.

When everyone thinks they have seen it all, the front passenger side opens. The beautiful Winnie, wearing a tailored skirt suit and a headscarf in black, green and yellow, comes out.

Her hand in a fist, she looks at the crowd, smiles charmingly, then raises the fist and says fiercely, '*Amandla.*' Power.

Nelson comes and stands beside her, holds her waist and joins the crowd as they raise their fists and respond to her, '*Awethu.*' It's ours.

An unanticipated applause and cheering starts from the crowd. Winnie and Nelson look at each other tenderly, but then Sergeant Vorster interrupts the moment.

'Mandela,' he says to Nelson.

'That's Mr Mandela to you, Sergeant. How can I help you?'

Vorster looks at him with disdain. His thoughts are mirrored on his face. Cheeky native, he is thinking. One day we will get you.

What he says instead is, 'Move that car. This is not a parking area.'

'Or what, Sergeant?' Mandela asks. 'Are you going to arrest me?'

It's almost as though the two men are about to come to blows.

But the doors to the court open and everyone's attention goes there.

Vorster still manages one last victory. He gently but firmly shoves Winnie away from Nelson. 'The defendants cannot be with civilians,' he says authoritatively.

Winnie holds out her hand to Nelson. He just manages to squeeze it and mouths, 'Courage, s'thandwa sam',' before Vorster successfully separates them.

As Issy Maisels leads him and the other defendants into the synagogue that has been converted into a courtroom, Nelson wonders whether that could be the last time he touches his wife's hand.

It would be very painful if it was.

A squeeze of the fingers in a crowd, broken up by a policeman.

He feels a nudge in his side. He looks beside him, and there he is.

Walter.

Nelson does not know where Walter came from.

Walter whispers to him, 'Amandla, Nelson.' Walter has a way of sensing when someone is down.

Nelson's mood is immediately uplifted. 'Awethu,' he answers. The power is theirs. The final thirty defendants in a trial that began in 1956 with 156 defendants.

The rest of them have been acquitted, and Nelson hopes the same will happen to them today.

They should be thirty-one. But one of them is missing. Well, not missing. Nelson knows where he is.

Bechuanaland.

He remembers how Wilton Mkwayi came to be absent.

On another trial date, much like today, another policeman with the same overzealousness of Vorster released Wilton. He did not mean to do it, of course. It really was a case of incompetence meeting zeal.

That day, the court had been adjourned earlier than usual. Wilton, one of the defendants, had got separated from the other defendants as they headed out. They always sat alphabetically by last name, so Nelson remembers seeing Wilton being herded off by the police. Despite having bail, the police had decided to re-arrest the defendants outside the gate as they looked for transport.

Wilton walked up to one of the policemen and enquired, 'What's going on?' His voice was very distinctive, so Nelson heard him.

The policeman probably thought he was a journalist from *Drum* magazine because he said to him, '*Voetsek*, Native. Just go.'

Wilton tried to tell him that he was part of the men and women on trial, but the policeman wasn't listening.

'Hey hey, I don't want trouble. What?' the policeman asked.

'I'm one of the accused,' Nelson heard Wilton answer.

'Liar, you keep standing here and I will arrest you for obstruction of justice,' he threatened.

So Wilton left.

Nelson hopes that they do not get convicted, but if they do, he hopes that some policeman can make the same mistake that they did with Wilton.

Then he smiles ruefully. Fat chance of *that* happening. Out of all the thirty defendants still left, his face is probably one of the few faces that even the least observant policeman will remember.

The defendants are seated.

Supporters and journalists are pressed at the door.

When the Old Synagogue doors finally open, many are turned away but the court is still packed.

Nelson and the other twenty-nine accused are seated alphabetically. They rise as the three judges who will give judgement in their case walk in.

They consist of Justice Rumpff, who Nelson remembers from when he judged the 1952 Defiance Trial. From his performance then and throughout this lengthy trial, Justice Rumpff has appeared to be led by the letter of the law rather than the desires of the prosecution or the defendants. Nelson has faith in their defence team. He hopes the judges were equally impressed.

The second judge is Justice Simon Bekker. Throughout the trial, his wife has collected goods to bring to the accused to sustain them. He hopes that her sympathy for them results in some influence on her husband to show the same.

The final judge is Justice Kennedy, who couldn't help but be impressed when Dr Wilson Nconco testified for the defence. When Dr Nconco, in response to the defence's questions to him to show him as a credible witness, mentioned his achievements, Justice Kennedy loudly and proudly proclaimed in isiZulu, '*Sinjalo thina maZulu.*' We are like that, we Zulus. Nelson hopes this outburst declaring the white Justice's self-identification as a Zulu will stand in their good stead.

When all are seated, Justice Rumpff reads the judgement:

'It has not been proved that, over the indictment period, the African National Congress had, as a matter of policy, decided to use violence as a method to achieve its ends, or to establish a form of state having the fundamental attributes of a Marxist-Leninist state.'

The thirty, who are standing as the judgement is read, have been holding hands. At this juncture, they each squeeze the hand of the next person tightly. Dare they hope?

He continues, 'The accused are accordingly found *not guilty* and are discharged.'

Would the judges have given a different verdict if they had known that among the thirty of them, some are already talking about an armed revolution? Nelson wonders. But he smiles in relief.

The court erupts.

The audience ululates, applauds and whistles in celebration.

The accused hug each other and pump hands. For them, it has been an exhausting five years. Some of them have lost incomes. Others have been estranged from their families, but they have also become closer and created new bonds with their fellow accused.

The prosecution team packs their files stoically. They cross over to the defence team and shake hands. They are not too worried. They are sure to get the skelems sooner or later, and they will get a death sentence for them or a life term. Especially that pair, Nelson and Walter, who think they are such clever blacks. And Slovo and his wife Ruth – bloody Communists.

The defence team of ten lawyers, led by Issy Maisels, is hoisted on the shoulders of the accused as they proceed out. This is particularly comical when it comes to Issy Maisels who is not exactly slender.

When they get outside, the now free men and women join the crowd in singing a rousing rendition of *Nkosi Sikelel' iAfrika*.

Winnie walks over to Nelson. A brief reunion before they are parted. He separates himself from his comrades and meets her halfway. He kisses her.

'Do you realize,' she says to him, a little loudly so he can hear as there is much noise from everyone around them, 'do you realize that this is the first time you have been a free man since we got married?'

He smiles and acknowledges the truth of her words; indeed it has.

'And do you realize,' he says sorrowfully, 'that despite my being a free man, I am still not free to come home to you and the children?'

She hugs him and puts his face in her hands. 'Nelson, I knew who you were and the sacrifices it would mean when I married you.'

He shakes his head. 'You knew you were marrying an activist, s'thandwa. You knew he may sometimes be away from home. You had an idea that that home – our home, 8115 Vilakazi Street in Orlando West Extension, in Soweto – may be raided by police. But I doubt you knew you would have to be mother *and* father to our children.'

She kisses him and says, 'I do now and we will be fine, Nelson. A wise man told me some wise words today and I would like to share them with you.'

'What did this wise man tell you and why is the wise man busy sharing words with my wife?' Nelson asks with a fake growl.

Winnie always knows how to bring out the playful side in her husband just as easily as she does the serious revolutionary side of him. She laughs loudly, throwing her head back. It's a joyous laugh that starts in her belly, bubbles up, and then lights her eyes before it bursts out of her mouth.

Nelson can't help it. He joins his wife in the laughter.

He cannot remember when he laughed like this. The laughter of a free man.

Every time he catches her eyes, they start laughing again. It is as though, in this sea of humanity, they have created their own island.

'So what did the wise man tell you?'

She sobers up, puts her hands on each side of his face again, looks him in the eyes and says, 'Courage, s'thandwa sam'.'

He holds her then. Holds her like he will never let her go. He does not want to. But he has to.

They separate and the rest of the world comes into view.

'We are going to Joe and Ruth's to celebrate the judgement. Nelson and Winnie, are you joining us?' Lillian – another of the accused celebrating her freedom – asks.

Winnie replies, 'I have to go back to the children. Have fun, and congratulations.'

'Sharp comrade, Winnie. See you soon,' Lillian says, giving Winnie the Congress thumbs-up sign and then turning her attention to Nelson. 'Wena ke, Nelson?'

'I wish I could, Lillian, but there is some work the movement requires of me.'

Walter gives him the thumbs-up sign and Nelson returns it. He kisses and hugs Lillian in celebration of their shared victory, then kisses Winnie. He looks at her as though drinking her in so he can remember her face in the uncertain underground, as he is unsure when he will see her next.

He wishes he could go to the victory party. That he could share a drink or three with his comrades on being free. But he doesn't trust the system. This judgement has humiliated the government on the global stage. They will be trying to strike back. He wouldn't put it past them to raid the party. He knows they have spies everywhere.

He looks at Winnie again and mouths, 'I love you.' She may be his comrade, but she is also his love and the mother to his two youngest children.

On this first day of freedom after a lengthy judgement, Nelson knows he is still not really free until apartheid and minority rule are defeated. He can never be free when so many who look like him are slaves to the apartheid system.

He gets in a different car from the one he arrived in. A car that is so common no one will remember it. He looks at Winnie again longingly as his comrade drives them off to Johannesburg, to an address that only this driver seems to know. When will he see her again?

4

The time comes in the life of any nation when there remains only two choices: **submit or fight!**

THAT TIME has now come to **South Africa!**

LOSS OF A TERRORIST

In Johannesburg on 17th April, the sun shines brightly. But Sergeant Vorster's day is about to get dark. The policeman who is supposed to guard Mandela – Constable Coetzee – walks into the office of five with his shoulders slumped.

'What? What has that trouble-making native done now?' Vorster asks. He is ready to arrest that Mandela if he has broken any laws.

He can't arrest him.

'We have lost him,' Coetzee tells him.

'What do you mean, you have lost him? How do you lose an African who is over six feet tall in a country of short Africans? What is wrong with you?'

'Askies,' Coetzee answers awkwardly.

Askies? Sorry? Is that all he has to say? 'Do you know what that means? How this can get us—' But before Sergeant Vorster finishes, the phone on his desk rings. It's his uncle, John Vorster. Minister of Justice.

'A native is cleverer than you and your team?' he says. Uncle Honourable Minister is angry. He has not bothered with any politeness or even to greet his nephew. How did he know? Vorster wonders. He, Sergeant Vorster, has only found out about Mandela's disappearance a few minutes ago.

'*Oom?* Uncle?' Vorster says. He is hoping that bringing some familial feeling will guarantee that his uncle is kinder to him.

'Don't *oom* me, son. You and your team have messed up on this. How did this happen, nephew?'

And now Vorster wishes his uncle had not reminded him of the family ties, although he started it. He feels like he has let down the family. These natives are not clever enough to escape. Not even Mandela. He has a feeling he knows how it happened. He tells his Uncle John what he thinks.

'I am pretty sure it's the native sympathizers, sir. The agents of Russia. The Jewish Communists. First, they tried to kill the Prime Minister and now they are hiding this Mandela. Ja. That's what they are doing,' Sergeant Vorster says with what he hopes is conviction.

'I don't care who or what,' the Minister yells down the line. 'Find that trouble-making native.

Find Mandela. Have *Wanted* adverts placed in every newspaper in the country, and in every village.' Then the Minister lowers his voice. 'And, son?'

'Yes, Honourable Minister,' Sergeant Vorster says with a touch of fear in his voice.

The Minister lowers his voice, barely above a whisper. 'Your grandfather – my father – always said you were not very clever. I always defended you.' Then he raises his voice, yells again and the whole of Sergeant Vorster's office stops what they are doing to listen. 'Don't let me agree with my father – find that Mandela. NOW.'

As Sergeant Vorster is about to respond, he realizes that his uncle has already hung up. Sweat is dripping down his face. His hand holding the telephone is sweaty and he is holding onto the handset tightly.

'What are you all looking at? You heard the man. Find Mandela.' Everyone continues to lurk around quietly as though trying to decide what to do. 'What are you waiting for? *Now!*' he yells again, just like his uncle on the phone. There is a flurry of activity in the office.

But … maybe this is not the way to do it, he thinks. He needs a better strategy.

'All right, everyone. Gather around, please?'

The policemen come over to Vorster's desk hesitantly. They are not used to this level of politeness. Among them is the policeman who has been on Mandela duty. Constable Coetzee.

'So what happened? How did you lose him?'

And the young policeman explains to everyone. He followed Mandela to Joe and Ruth's house yesterday late afternoon. He was not wearing a uniform and was in an unmarked car. He watched the gate the whole night. 'Except...' he says with some hesitation.

'Except when?' Sergeant Vorster wants to know. The other three policemen nod to encourage him to go on.

'Well, there was a time that Ruth came over.' He sounds hesitant.

'And?'

'Last night. It was 22:43 hours. I had just looked at my wristwatch. She knocked on my car window, like so.' He imitates her knocking, using Vorster's desk.

'Go on.'

'She was holding a flask of coffee and cake and she said, "Officer. It's getting chilly out here. I brought you some coffee and cake while you wait."'

There is a collective groan from the other policemen.

'What? I don't know how she knew. I was in an unmarked car and I wasn't wearing uniform, but when she showed she thought I may be working for the police, I thought it was a kind gesture. Liberals are generally not kind to us. They hate us.'

Vorster puts his right hand in a fist, then punches into his left hand. He wishes he could punch this policeman. 'What is wrong with you? Is there something wrong with your mind?' he asks while poking the policeman's head.

'No, sir. I just thought—'

'You are not paid to think, Coetzee. Or to eat cake and coffee from Communists. Are you also a Communist now?' Vorster questions.

'No, sir. It's just that it was so cold and it was so kind,' the policeman says miserably.

'You could have been poisoned. How did you find out that Mandela was gone?' Vorster wants to know.

'This morning. The Slovos' maid came and knocked on my window. She had come to get the plate and coffee flask and cup from the car. And she said to me, "Mr Joe told me to tell you that you can leave now. Mr Mandela left last night."' He puts his face in his hands, feeling as though he has really let the team down. He wants to cry.

Vorster slaps him painfully on the back. 'Son, there will be no tears here. Instead, let's find a way to fix this.' And then he issues his orders. 'When Sergeant Marwa comes, I want you and him to design a *Wanted* poster. I want it translated in all the languages of this country for all the newspapers and radio stations. We are going to catch Mandela and he will wish he could get coffee and cake in the stocks.'

The other police are given various duties. One is put on telephone duty. Vorster instructs him to call all the police stations across the countries and let them know that Nelson Mandela is on the *Wanted* list. Mandela tries to be a clever native, so if they catch him he is sure he will ask them, 'On what charges?' If they get Mandela, the police must therefore tell him whatever charge that will allow them to arrest him and then bring Mandela to Johannesburg.

He, Sergeant Vorster, is going to prove to his uncle, the Minister, that his grandfather was wrong. He is clever and he can catch even the cleverest of natives. He takes his jacket from the back of the chair. It's ten o'clock in the morning, but what he needs right now is a double brandy.

This Mandela has put him in a bad mood, and he will ensure the man suffers when he finally gets him. He walks out of the office while the rest of the police do their best to look busy.

5

TOUGH CAMPAIGN AND CLOSE CALLS

I t has been weeks driving cross-country as chief campaigner for the movement. It is as though every new town Nelson gets into has more *Wanted* posters with an image of him than the one before. Members of the movement have been useful. Mothers have taught their children well, and in families with Welcome Dover coal-fired stoves, the children bring the posters home to help start the fires in the stoves.

Nelson is putting in whatever work he can to ensure that from 29th May to the 31st, enough people take part in a stay-at-home protest against the declaration of Republic Day on 31st May. If the apartheid government believes only white voices matter in deciding the future of the country, the movement believes a successful stay-at-home protest will show them that their economy cannot function without the Africans, Indians and Coloureds.

Nelson, their chief campaigner, is not as hopeful as the leaders of the movement though. He has been to Durban and Pietermaritzburg. To Port Elizabeth and to Cape Town. And to many small towns in between. Every now and again the question has come up: 'Does he think another peaceful stay-away will make a difference?' People tell him about being the only breadwinners in their families. 'If we stay away and we lose our jobs, how will the movement help us?'

Nelson does not have a satisfactory answer. There are many, too, who think peaceful protests are past their sell-by date. 'When,' one young man asks in Durban, 'will the movement train us and give us arms so we can fight the Boers man to man? Other organizations have started doing military training.'

Nelson is a little irritated. He knows the reference to other organizations is really a reference to the Pan African Congress that broke away from the ANC. Still a small organization, but lately a thorn in the flesh, as it always makes the ANC movement appear to be timid and out of touch with the people. He does not know how to respond.

The question of the young man is echoed in a meeting with clergymen in a Cape Town township. It is at the beginning of this meeting, that in an opening prayer, Nelson hears it again.

The minister prays, 'Thank you, Lord, for your bounty and goodness, for your mercy and for your concern for all men.' The minister looks at each and every man who is kneeling.

The men open their eyes, thinking he is done, but maybe the minister just wants whoever he is speaking to or praying with to note those who are with him. To be a witness to this moment.

He continues, admonishing his God. 'Remember, Lord, that some of your subjects are more downtrodden than others. Because, you see, it sometimes appears as though you aren't paying attention. And if you don't show a little more initiative in leading the black nation to salvation, Lord,' the Minister continues, 'the black nation will have to take matters into their own hands. Amen.'

Nelson echoes 'Amen' with everyone else, and again asks himself whether these stay-away campaigns that he is encouraging people to take part in will be fruitless. In his mind, he is battling with himself. What if he thinks more and more people want an armed struggle just because he and his comrades have discussed it? The majority of the people in the country are peaceful people. Would *they* want that?

As he travels, he takes each and every opportunity to convert one more person to take part in the stay-at-home campaign. On his last morning in Cape Town, he thanks the Coloured manager of the hotel he has been staying in. The manager is gracious. 'Before you go, sir,' the manager asks politely, 'would you mind answering a question for me?'

'Absolutely, my brother.' Nelson, who was walking away, turns back to the manager.

'It's just… Mr Mandela,' he says, sounding a little hesitant.

Nelson is taken aback by the use of his name. He had checked in under another name. He walks closer to the reception desk. Then he sees it. A handful of posters with his face on it. This manager would have been blind not to see that it's him. He can only hope that because he was booked in by a member of the movement, this manager will not say anything. 'Yes?' Nelson says encouragingly.

'Some in the Coloured community are worried,' the manager says. 'We are neither white nor black.' He pauses, and Nelson nods to tell him to go on. 'Isn't there a danger that when a majority government – which will of course be African, because the Africans are the majority – comes into power, we will suffer the same discrimination that we do under white people but in reverse?' he says.

'Why do you think that?' Nelson asks.

'Well sir, respectfully, your party is called the African National Congress. It doesn't seem like it includes any other races,' he answers matter-of-factly.

Nelson goes into lecture mode and tells him about non-racialism. He tells the manager about their alliance with Indians and whites and Coloureds. Indeed, it's an official from the South African Coloured People's Organization, George Peake, who had booked him into the hotel and has now come to pick him up. 'Because you see,' Nelson ends, 'the first words in the Freedom Charter are "*South Africa belongs to all who live in it*", and those are as important as any other words in that document.'

The manager's face lights up as comprehension dawns. Why don't the guys from Khayelitsha and Langa explain this African National Congress just as well? he wonders.

Nelson has other worries. If this manager could identify him, many other people are likely to, and next time it might not be someone of goodwill. He needs to do better. Consider disguises. He needs to look more like an average black man in his current South Africa.

When he gets back to Johannesburg that is exactly what he does. He walks less tall so he doesn't attract attention. When he is spoken to, he doesn't look at anyone straight in the face as he generally would. Rather, he keeps his head low, a little tilted to the side, eyes lowered but not so much as to look dishonest; rather, to appear respectful. As though he is agreeing to whatever the speaker is saying.

He moves from one flat to another as he helps to organize for the three-day stay-away. Mostly he dresses as a chef, gardener or chauffeur. He uses the chef disguise sometimes when undercover in friends' places that have guests coming. The guests never pay attention to him when passing him, not when he is wearing his chef's uniform. As a gardener, he wears overalls and round, rimless glasses. He walks with a shuffle and speaks only when spoken to. The clueless, affable native of many a white man's belief.

His favourite disguise is as a chauffeur, though. When in this disguise, he wears a dustcoat and a cap, so he appears as though he is waiting for his baas.

Sometimes he takes on other disguises, depending on where he wants access. He has been a messenger, a mine worker, a labourer. Newspapers often fill up their front pages with false claims of where he has been seen across the country. These same newspapers have now given him the nickname 'The Black Pimpernel' after the fictional hero of Baroness Orczy's novel, *The Scarlet Pimpernel*. It amuses Nelson as much as it annoys him. Therein lies the racism of this country, even among newspapers that consider themselves liberal. To them, he can't just be Nelson Mandela of South Africa. He has to be a black version of something white for them to make sense of it. Of him.

His disguises are not yet perfect, though. In his chauffeur's uniform in Johannesburg's central business district, he sees a policeman he recognizes. It's Marwa: Sergeant Maxwell Levy Marwa. Nelson saw him at the rally taking notes and talking to Sergeant Vorster. He knows they work together. He has been told that Marwa has also been seen in the company of Coetzee: the man who lost sight of him from outside Ruth and Joe's home, with the help of Ruth.

This time, Sergeant Marwa walks towards him in a very deliberate manner. He is looking straight at Nelson as he plays with the handcuffs at his side. Nelson tries to look around to see whether there is a place he can run to. His goose is cooked, he thinks.

Before he can run though, Sergeant Marwa, now so close, smiles at him and pretends he is wiping his face. Then the policeman mumbles without seeming to open his mouth, but words that Nelson can hear, 'They got your letter. Verwoerd is furious.' Then he acts like he is rubbing his face. 'There will be a big raid on the 2nd and 3rd of May. Stay away from any of your comrades.'

As Sergeant Marwa takes away his hands from his face, he gives the movement's thumbs-up sign and continues patrolling.

Nelson is relieved. He was planning to sneak to his home and see his wife and children tomorrow. But he will have to make another plan.

A HOMELY INTERLUDE

Marwa warned and it has come to pass. As Nelson continues with his underground life and the campaign, the largest raid to date happens on the night of 2nd May and the early hours of 3rd May. He hears about it from Winnie when he next sees her.

It's been too long since he last saw her. He has not seen her since that day at the court as he drove away. It had been too risky. Then he had left the city. Then there were raids as per Marwa's information.

But today he is going to 8115 Vilakazi Street, Orlando West Extension in Soweto. Today, he will go home again – his first time since he left back before he knew the results of the Treason Trial. Ruth is driving him there, and they both hope that she will not get stopped. But if she does, she has a press pass and is

allowed in the township. They pray that no one will search her car – he is hiding in the boot of the car, covered by some newspapers. A difficult mission for a man who is fifteen centimetres short of two metres, but desperate times call for desperate measures.

They make it without being stopped. When they arrive that late afternoon, Ruth parks as close to the kitchen as possible, as though they are about to unload something heavy. They are. But if anyone knew what or who it was, they could be in serious trouble with the apartheid police.

'Ruth,' Winnie says loudly, pretending to be surprised, 'why didn't you say you were coming? What a pleasant surprise!' With her is Nelson's sister Mabel who has been staying with Winnie and helping with the two children.

'Winnie. Mabel, how good to see you. I had to go and double-check something on a story with the police, so I thought I should drop by.' If anyone heard her, they will not go and report to the police. After all, Ruth has just come from the police station.

Zenani and Zindziswa come outside. 'Zeni, take your baby sister inside and go and play with the dollies in the bedroom,' Winnie tells them.

'Can we play in your bedroom, Mama?' Zenani asks.

Winnie needs her to leave. 'Yes, Zeni. You can play in my bedroom.' She knows it will look disastrous

when they are done with it, but anything to get them out of the way…

'And can we put lipstick on the dollies, Mama?'

'Of course, my baby, now go on.' Winnie sighs.

Satisfied, Zenani holds her little sister's hand, walks into the kitchen, past the living-cum-dining room and then right into the master bedroom of this two-bedroom house. As Winnie and Mabel expect, she closes the door, meaning that they are about to get into some mischief. It suits the adults just fine.

Ruth opens the boot of the car. Nelson gets out and crouch-runs into the house. With him safely in the house, Ruth locks up the car.

'Thank you so much for coming by, Ruth. Won't you come in for tea?' Winnie says politely.

'I really wish I could, my dear, but I must get home before it's too late. The girls are waiting for me. I promised them we would bake some muffins,' Ruth replies.

'That's unfortunate. Well, see you soon, and next time please warn me so I can have baked.'

Ruth kisses Mabel, then kisses Winnie and whispers, 'Kathy will come and pick him up early tomorrow.' Kathy is the nickname for the anti-apartheid activist Ahmed Kathrada.

Winnie speaks loudly, 'Drive safely, Ruth.'

Winnie goes into the house with Mabel close behind. Nelson stands there and looks at her. Then he takes her in his arms. 'S'thandwa. I have missed you so much.' He holds his head back and looks at her face. She looks even more beautiful than when he last remembered her. Is that possible or is it his imagination?

'And I, I have missed you too, Nelson. It's good to have you home, albeit briefly.'

'It's good to *be* home.' Then he kisses her. Mabel clears her throat loudly and both Nelson and Winnie start giggling. Nelson turns to her and says, 'Hawu, sisi. I can't even say hello to my wife for five minutes?'

Mabel chuckles. 'It looked like you were preparing to take longer than that to say hello to your wife.'

Brother and sister exchange pleasantries. Then Nelson walks to the bedroom and opens the door. Zindziswa is the first to see him. She starts crying.

Zeni, who has been busy putting powder on her face, turns but her reaction is different. She remembers her father and she runs over to him. 'Tata.'

He scoops the elder girl in his arms, and then Zindzi follows cautiously and asks, 'Tata?'

'Yes, nana. It's your tata.' Then he scoops her in the other arm. 'Now what are you playing at here?'

For the next few hours, as Winnie prepares supper and Mabel does the ironing, this big man – the apartheid government's most wanted man – spends time with his daughters which is filled with laughter and love. They use their mother's make-up to paint his face.

68

When Winnie calls them for dinner, she howls with laughter and calls Mabel to come and see. Mabel joins in the laughter.

After dinner, Nelson is happy to enjoy what others may consider as ordinary but what he feels is a special time with his family. He delights at telling the girls a bedtime story, with one of them seated on each of his knees. He thrills at hearing Zeni ask, 'Tell us another one, tata,' and an echo from Zindzi, 'Ewe, tata. Tell us anada.' And even though he is tired and has a long day ahead tomorrow, he indulges them, because who knows when next he will be with them again? Not him.

When his sister Mabel, the girls' Aunt Mabel, tries to tell the two girls it's time for bed, they refuse to go. 'We are not tired,' they say.

It breaks Nelson's heart. He can see the pain echoed in Winnie's smile even as she smiles bravely. The girls are trying to hold onto every last minute they can with him. Within a quarter of an hour though, they nod off, right there while sitting on his knees. He lifts both of them and tucks them in the bed they share. He kisses them goodnight and Zeni opens her eyes and asks drowsily, 'Goodnight, tata. See you tomorrow.'

'Goodnight, baby.'

He won't lie to her that he will see her tomorrow. By the time she wakes up, he will have long gone. Kathy is picking him up early in the morning.

'Goodnight, child of our home,' his sister says, as she goes to the bedroom with the girls.

He puts his hands on her shoulders and looks at her: his little sister, but his wife's older sister. 'Thank you, our sister. Thank you for looking after our children and our wife.'

She smiles then and kisses him. A smile that brightens her face and makes her look a decade younger than she is. 'Be safe,' she says.

Winnie has two glasses of whisky on the table. She hands him a glass and clinks it with hers. 'Welcome home, s'thandwa,' she says.

He takes a gulp and smiles. 'If coming home guarantees that I always see your beautiful face and drink such good whisky then, s'thandwa, I shall find a way of doing it more often.'

He does not know how wrong he is. It's the last time he will be home in a long long time.

7

The time comes in the life of any nation when there remains only two choices: **submit or fight!**

THAT TIME has now come to **South Africa!**

TOWARDS ARMED REVOLUTION

On the evening of 29th May, Nelson drives the man he stays with to a neighbourhood about thirty minutes away from where they are staying. There, using a telephone booth on a side street, he calls one of the newspapers sympathetic to the movement.

Today was the first day of the movement's three-day campaign action. Today, the country and the movement learn that the people are tired of peaceful protests. The stay-away was unsuccessful.

Nelson, through his interview, calls off the action for the remaining two days. It is the pragmatic action for any leader to take so that the organization does not have too much egg on its face.

With this failure, and in chats with Walter and his other comrades, Nelson decides that at the next meeting he shall suggest they move to an armed struggle. Walter agrees that this is the way to go. He and Walter have talked about this move since the early Fifties. And yet, when they have the meeting, it doesn't turn out quite as Nelson expects it to.

When he brings it up for discussion, a member of the leadership – Moses Kotane – opposes it. The two argue for their positions eloquently. When Nelson argues, most of those listening are convinced that they will take his side. But when the other speaker starts mentioning his points, everyone agrees with him. Finally, the discussion is put to a vote. There is no one on Nelson's side. Not even Walter.

Nelson is hurt. Walter is his guy, his friend, his boy, his ride or die. How could he betray him like that and not take his side? He would have been OK with everyone else, but... Walter? Come on.

So he turns to Walter as soon as they are alone and says quietly, but with a lot of anger, 'You too? You couldn't be on my side?'

Walter smiles and responds, 'You know I am with you on the armed struggle, but Moses made such an important speech it wouldn't have been easy to defeat him. My vote then was deliberate, so that I wouldn't antagonize him. But listen. I will sort it out.'

'How?' Nelson asks. He can't imagine how Walter will fix this.

'I will organize a one-on-one meeting between

you two. You become the good lawyer you are and convince him.'

Nelson is still unhappy but he nods. It's worth a try.

A week later, he meets up with Moses at a meeting set up by Walter. As the two men with opposing positions speak, Walter is helping Moses's wife in the kitchen. Raised by his Xhosa mother and with a family of his own, Walter is handy in the kitchen and it is he who bakes the scones that shall be served at tea later that afternoon as Moses's wife makes lunch.

At lunchtime, Moses has not yet changed his position. He and Nelson agree to call a truce so that they can eat lunch without making the rest of the people speak politics. They talk of other things. Later, much later, Walter brings the two men some scones. One of Moses's sons is holding the tea tray.

When Moses takes his first bite of the scone, his face looks angelic. For two minutes while he eats the scone, he says nothing and points at Nelson to keep quiet. After he finishes the scone, he takes a few sips of tea. When he finally puts down his teacup, he turns to Walter and says, 'Did you bake that? Because I know no one in this house can bake like that.'

Walter smiles. 'A small family recipe that my mother taught me.'

'I am a Communist and don't believe in God, but Jesus, that was the best baking I have ever tasted,' Moses says with a big grin on his face. Then he says to

Walter, 'So you, Walter? What do you think? Should we get into an armed struggle?'

Walter shrugs his shoulders. 'I think Nelson is right, you know? Our people are tired of peaceful protests that still result in their getting fired at work or, worse, shot at.'

'Have you always felt this way, Walter?' Moses asks.

'Well, I have to tell you, Nelson and I have discussed this for a long time and, yes, I have felt this way for a while.'

'So why didn't you say anything at the meeting to support Nelson last week?' Moses wants to know.

There is a twinkle in Walter's brown eyes and a smile on his face when he answers, 'Because, Moses, you had not yet eaten my scones.'

They all laugh as Nelson joins in the tea-and-scone routine. A little while later however, when Walter and Nelson suggest they have to leave, Moses gets serious.

'You two did some nice tag-teaming there. And you know, I think I can be swayed to share your position.' Then he ends, 'I don't promise anything, Nelson, but bring it up at the next committee meeting and we'll see what happens.'

They both have a good feeling about their position as they leave Moses and his family to the scones that Walter baked. Nelson is driving, with Walter on the passenger seat. They stop at a traffic light – a robot, as it is commonly called – and a car pulls up next to him on the right.

A police car.

Inside the car, on the passenger seat, is Sergeant Vorster. Nelson is not a praying man but now he says a silent prayer. 'God, please don't let them look this side. If I manage to escape this,' he promises, as does everyone in trouble, 'I will go to church at least once every three months.'

Sergeant Vorster looks over at the car on his left. Nelson can feel Vorster's eyes on him so he looks straight ahead. 'Walter, Vorster is in the car next to us,' he tells Walter, while continuing to look ahead.

'Man, oh man. If there is a white man who can actually recognize you, it's Sergeant Vorster,' Walter says nervously.

But the lights change and the police car moves forward at top speed.

Today was Nelson's lucky day. He has managed to change Moses's position on non-violence, and it looks like Sergeant Vorster did not recognize him. Both he and Walter heave sighs of relief at the same time, then start laughing nervously. The laughter moves from nervousness to delirious-sounding.

That was a close call.

8

TESTING, TESTING

Nelson had been worried but now, thanks to Moses' support, the movement has agreed that he can set up a military wing. He knows it will not be easy. Orders from the top are that, whatever he does, his activities with the armed wing should not get in the way of whatever duties he is assigned for the movement.

He will need some people to help.

One day, he is with Joe and Walter in Wolfie Kodesh's bachelor pad, where he has been staying in between his trips around the country.

'A High Command, that's what we need,' Joe suggests. They have all just returned from Durban, where Nelson received the final permission to set up the wing.

'I was reading some books on military action and

that's what you should call the team that will help you,' Joe finishes his train of thought.

'What does "High Command" even mean?' Walter asks. 'It sounds like something that's bigger than what we will actually have.'

Nelson says excitedly, 'But that's the point, isn't it, Walter? We may be starting small and without any knowledge of weapons, but by the time we are done learning all there's to learn, we will be a formidable army and we will crush the apartheid regime until they come crawling to us to negotiate,' he says, punching his right fist in his left hand. He pauses, then adds dreamily, 'And I, Nelson Rolihlahla Mandela shall be Commander-in-Chief of this soon-to-be formidable army and you, Walter and Joe, will be part of the High Command.'

They shake each other's hands vigorously and they laugh. This is finally going to happen. They are going to have an army.

'We will recruit South Africans of different races, religions and ages who believe in freedom and justice for all,' Joe says with enthusiasm.

Nelson shakes his head. 'Well, maybe everything else but not different ages. Can you imagine someone who is the same age as our Chief Luthuli trying to run away after planting an explosive in a strategic place?'

They all find this funny and laugh loudly again, but then Nelson quietens down first and asks, 'But what are we going to call the organization? It needs a different name so that whatever we do is not associated with the movement.'

They all look at each other as they try to figure out names.

'How about *AmaQhawe eNkululeko*?' Nelson suggests.

'Say that again… *Ka ka*, and what does it mean?' Joe asks.

Nelson answers slowly, '*Ah-mah-Qha-weh e-Nkoo-loo-leh-koh*. It means "Heroes of Freedom". Which is what we would be. Is it the click in *Qha* that's making it tough for you, Joe?'

Walter shakes his head, 'I think it's a problematic name, Nelson. If Joe, who is part of your High Command, can't pronounce the name of the organization, isn't the battle half lost already?'

Nelson shrugs his shoulders. 'Do you have something better?'

'As a matter of fact, I think I do,' Walter says.

Both Nelson and Joe look at him and say together, 'What?

'*Oom-kho-nto weh-see-zwe*,' Walter says slowly, spelling it out. Then he smiles. '*umkhonto we Sizwe*. Joe, it means "Spear of the Nation". We are not coming to shield the nation. We are coming to fight for it, and a spear is a traditional weapon in this country known to cause harm,' Walter ends.

'*uMkhonto we Sizwe,*' Joe repeats. 'There are no clicks. Even I can say it.'

'*uMkhonto we Sizwe* it is then, although, Joe,' Nelson says with a teasing grin on his face, 'we may have to think twice about your citizenship in a free South Africa if you can't make an effort to speak any of the native languages beyond saying "*uMkhonto we Sizwe*".'

They hear footsteps outside and all three of them keep quiet. They look around, but apart from the wardrobe there is nowhere to hide. If the police were to break down the door, their army will end before it has even begun.

There are two short knocks on the door. A pause and another knock.

Joe and Walter look at Nelson questioningly. Nelson exhales. He mouths, 'It's Wolfie.' They all relax and Nelson opens the door.

'Comrades.' Wolfie walks in with a big grin. 'Welcome back from Durban.'

They brief Wolfie on the decision that has been taken. It is his home, but Nelson asks him to excuse them as the High Command, so that they can discuss the structure the new organization will take.

'That's fine. I need to go and buy you comrades some food and drinks anyway. An hour? Two hours?'

'Two hours is perfect,' Nelson answers.

The High Command considers four approaches to how they will fight against the regime: sabotage, guerrilla warfare, terrorism and open revolution.

They immediately decide against terrorism as it would undermine any public sympathies if there should be needless loss of life. In a country as heavily militarized as theirs, open revolution would also lead to needless loss of soldiers and civilians.

Guerrilla warfare is a strong possibility, but as the ANC is still speaking non-violence, it wouldn't do to undertake it just yet to avoid conflict with the mother body. This leaves sabotage as the best alternative for the moment, but it does not stop those in the High Command from making plans for military training for their soldiers.

Different members come on board for carrying out the sabotage missions. Among them are some chemical engineer graduates and a pharmacist. Meanwhile, Nelson recruits Wolfie to become a soldier, and he forms part of the team Nelson travels with to test the very first explosives.

They are four in the car when they go to do the test: Nelson, Wolfie and two others, one of them a pharmacist. They are travelling to the east of Johannesburg, far away from the city in an unpopulated area that serves as a brickworks. There are some old and abandoned buildings in the space.

Nelson is driving, but his palms are sweaty. This is madness, he thinks. He is a father to five children. He has responsibilities. What does he think he is doing? he asks himself. When he parks, he rests his head on the steering wheel and exhales. His armpits are wet – he is still nervous – but at least they got here safely.

Wolfie, who is seated in the front seat, nudges him. 'We have company, comrade.'

Nelson panics and looks out. Please, no. Not the police? No. Not the police.

A security guard, who walks over to them purposefully. It could be trouble.

Nelson tells them all to get out of the car. He does the same. He then asks them to take out the equipment while he goes to chat to the security guard. As the others take out the equipment, they watch Nelson. He greets the security guard in isiZulu and then puts his hand on the security guard's shoulder. Nelson and the security guard chat for a while. None of them know what he says because they cannot understand isiZulu, but what they see is that the security guard walks away and he returns to them and tells them to proceed. Nelson informs them that he has convinced the man to let them stay.

Their first tests are simple. Bottles filled with petrol, closed with cloths dipped in more petrol which they light. Molotov cocktails. They test a few of these in one of the unused old buildings and every time the bottles burst into flame.

Nelson, who is the commander-in-chief of this operation, claps his hands excitedly. His enthusiasm is infectious and he soon has everyone else laughing and clapping their hands. After a few tests, they douse the fires and go out.

Outside, they prepare a tin of paraffin with a fuse made from the ink refill of a ballpoint pen inserted into the spout of the can. Into the refill the pharmacist has added specific chemicals to ensure an explosive reaction. They place the can into a pit and wait for twenty minutes. Nothing happens.

'Comrades, this is not good. What could have gone wrong?' Nelson asks.

'Let me go and get the tin in the pit. We may need to make some adjustments,' Wolfie bravely says.

'You are sure you don't want me to do it?' Nelson asks. It's the right question to ask. He is, after all, the commander-in-chief, even though of the four men, Wolfie is the only one without a wife and children.

Wolfie seems to be thinking this too because he says, 'No, Comrade Nelson. Let me do this,' and then goes down. He retrieves the tin from the pit, and the pharmacist makes some changes to it. Wolfie returns it to the pit and the other three men pull him out immediately after. A few seconds later, there is a blast from the pit, scattering a cloud of earth around them.

Success.

They get back to the car.

The commander-in-chief suggests some changes in the process but congratulates the team. Soon, very soon, the apartheid state will realize that they are in a state of war. And he, Nelson Mandela, will command the soldiers who will free the country from tyranny and lead them to freedom.

A SOLDIER DIES BUT ONCE

It feels good to know that things are going so well, Nelson thinks. It is this which informs his actions. Not only does he enlarge the High Command of *uMkhonto we Sizwe*, but he also finds a way to communicate with his comrades to set up sabotage teams in Cape Town, Port Elizabeth and Durban. The Durban team has, as its sabotage expert, a hard-drinking but passionate man, Bruno Mtolo. Having teams in more than one centre is the only way that the country and the world will notice when they set off the first explosions. Carefully worded messages will be dispatched by road, rail and public telephones at certain hours.

But Nelson and his High Command are also thinking beyond sabotage, even before the first sabotage actions have been undertaken. They have already organized and sent two recruits for military training in China. Wilton, the treason trialist who managed to escape, is also in China for military training.

At home, *uMkhonto we Sizwe* High Command has decided on their first date for sabotage.

Saturday 16th December is a Public Holiday in the apartheid government's calendar. The High Command has selected this day because it's the date that white South Africa celebrates the defeat of the Zulu King Dingane at the hands of the Afrikaners. Many Zulu warriors were killed on the day until the waters of a tributary of the Buffalo River turned red from their blood, giving the battle the name of the Battle of Blood River. The Afrikaners have since believed this means that God is on their side and they are supposed to be masters to the Africans. In selecting this date, then, the High Command hope to change the historical narrative and hit back.

Saturday 16th December, 1960 does not explode in quite the way the High Command had hoped it would. In Durban, the three bombs fail to explode. In Port Elizabeth, a sergeant hears an explosion in the direction of an electric substation. As he approaches the scene, he sees a group of men fleeing. One of them is caught by a white civilian and handed over to the sergeant. The other four men are never caught.

In Johannesburg, there is one success story. One of the comrades places a bomb on top of a telephone kiosk by a post office. It explodes. When he gets home, his wife asks him what happened. It's only then that he realizes that his eyebrows are singed, his hair is burnt and his suit has small burn holes in it.

In Soweto, a loud explosion is heard at the municipal offices in Dube at the same time as a man walks away from the building. The right side of the man's sleeve, just under the armpit, is burning and the left side of his head is blackened. His trousers are torn on the backside and there are burn marks. A police constable grabs the man. He leads the man to a tap to put the fire out. The constable removes the man's jacket and he sees injuries to his right wrist and right elbows. The constable then takes the man to the offices of the police behind the building. As a case is being opened, it occurs to the constable that he knows the man when he says his name – he had just failed to recognize him because of the damage done to his face by the explosion.

Another constable from Orlando police station joins them. Outside the gate and next to the pole, an African man lies dead with all the fingers and the palm of his hand blown off. Next to the body is a torn plastic container shaped like a bottle. The dead man is Petrus Molefe.

On its first day of operations, MK – as *uMkhonto we Sizwe* becomes known – has its first fatality in Petrus Molefe.

And its first two arrests: of the man who wore a burning jacket, and the other in Port Elizabeth.

A total of ten explosions are actually successful and recorded by the police. Five of them were in Johannesburg and the other five in Port Elizabeth.

At each place where there have been explosions, the MK has left a calling card. Their flyers.

They read in part:

The time comes in the life of any nation when there remains only two choices: submit or fight. That time has now come to South Africa. We shall not submit and we have no choice but to hit back by all means within our power in defence of our people, our future, our freedom…

When Minister John Vorster reads about the activities in the press the next day, Sergeant Vorster gets a phone call.

'Nephew, why have you still not caught Mandela? Why?'

'Uncle, I think we are close now.'

'Not good enough. You have been singing this same song for months. Can you catch Mandela or not?'

'I can, Uncle. I just need a little more time,' Sergeant Vorster says.

'We don't have time. I want Mandela. I want him found and in jail. If you do not catch that native or any of his comrades soon, I will make sure you are replaced, and you and your family can go and look after your grandfather at the farm.'

Just like before, the Honourable Minister hangs up on his nephew before Sergeant Vorster can answer. Everyone in that open office is looking at him.

'Maaaax!!!' Sergeant Vorster yells out to Sergeant Maxwell Levy Marwa. He is *not* going to move to the farm. His grandfather hates him and besides, he likes Johannesburg. What would he do on a farm?

Max walks over to him. 'I am right here. What is it, Sergeant?'

Why does Max always seem unbothered and so smug? Vorster wishes he could wipe the smugness of his face. 'Listen, we are in trouble. What do we know about the people who did this?'

Max shrugs. 'I heard something about someone who may be involved with these guys this morning.'

'What? What did you hear? Where is Mandela?' Vorster asks anxiously.

Max knows exactly where Mandela is. Less than twenty kilometres away. He says evasively, 'Last I heard from my informants who know his wife, he was in Cape Town. I think you should talk to the colleagues in Cape Town.'

Vorster looks relieved; less tense than when he got the phone call from his uncle. 'I will. I will talk to the guys in Cape Town. We will get Mandela, mark my words.'

Under his breath Max whispers, 'God forbid,' but loudly he says, 'Absolutely, Sergeant. Now let me go and do some paperwork.'

In an interview a day later, Justice Minister John Vorster says of the explosions, 'It's clear for me at this stage that white agitators are behind the sabotage that was committed on Saturday night in Johannesburg and Port Elizabeth.' In his mind he cannot imagine that the natives may be restless or, worse, restless enough to choose to push back.

On Christmas Eve, a newspaper reports that the Minister intends to introduce a sabotage bill in the next parliamentary session. This bill will include the death penalty.

Hearing this, Nelson ponders and consults with the High Command. They can either withdraw or continue to motivate people to fight on. They are at a fork in the road. If they choose to withdraw and dissolve MK, nothing will change. It will mean that Petrus Molefe died and those arrested were arrested for nothing.

'There is no turning back, comrades,' he says at the end of a meeting with the others in the High Command. 'Surrendering is not an option. My life, all our lives, are already death sentences in this hellhole. Because is lack of freedom not a form of death? Vorster, be damned. We will continue fighting on. The Spear of the Nation will not be blunted after the first thrust at the enemy. Amandla.'

His colleagues in the High Command respond bravely in strong voices, 'Awethu.'

10

The time comes in the life of any nation when there remains only two choices: **submit or fight!**

THAT TIME has now come to **South Africa!**

DISPLACEMENT AND REFUGE

The death of Petrus weighs over Nelson but more is to come. Under his command, sabotage missions begin to be carried out at police stations and government offices. Mostly without casualties, but not always. They also mine roads.

In Johannesburg, Sergeant Vorster is beginning to feel desperate. Will he ever catch The Black Pimpernel? He redoubles his efforts to track down Mandela.

Soon, Nelson feels he is in danger and one day a small slip means that he has to leave Wolfie's flat. It happens like this. Succumbing to his cravings for sour milk, Nelson buys some, and because there is limited space, he places the packet on the window's ledge.

Sitting and chatting quietly with Wolfie in the late afternoon, the blinds are closed as always but not

Nelson's ears. They overhear the voices of two men who must be gardeners at the flat talking in isiZulu.

'What is "our milk" doing on that ledge?' one of the men asks his companion.

'What do you mean "our milk"?' his companion asks.

'I mean amasi. White people don't drink amasi, mos. And it's a white man who stays there.'

The two men pause outside the window and seem to be examining the packet of sour milk.

'Do you think...?' the other man asks, but leaves the sentence hanging.

The other replies, 'Vele. White people don't drink this.'

They walk away.

As soon as their footsteps fade, Wolfie asks, 'What? What was that all about?'

'Not good.'

'What do you mean, *not good*? What did they say?'

'I need to leave, Wolfie. In this designated white suburb, those two men suspect that there is a black man staying here because you white men don't drink amasi.'

Wolfie slaps his forehead and says, 'Ja nee? How did we overlook such a small thing?'

Nelson won't allow Wolfie to blame himself for something he did. A good leader takes responsibility for their failures. 'It wasn't your fault, Wolfie. It was me. I got too relaxed. And perhaps this is a good thing because I would soon have got caught.'

Nelson can't help thinking that, although taking up residence there was a decision by those higher up in the movement, he has really enjoyed getting to know Wolfie. When he first arrived, he used to annoy Wolfie in the morning as he worked out. But now Wolfie wakes up and exercises with him. He will miss him.

They wait for it to become full night. Wolfie looks outside and, seeing no one, tells Nelson to come out.

A new hideout has been found. As Nelson walks out, he contemplates taking the amasi with him, but decides against it. If those two men are spies, this will only put Wolfie in trouble as it will show there was a black person in his home. Better for any police raid to find the amasi there and think Wolfie has gone native.

The man nicknamed The Black Pimpernel is wearing his chauffeur's outfit and jumps into the driver's side of the car. His companion goes to the passenger side. Nelson starts the engine. Their destination? A freehold property on the outskirts of Johannesburg with enough land for them not to be interrupted, or to hide what's necessary should anyone come to interrupt them.

Liliesleaf Farm. It will be the address that he stays at the most.

The apartheid operatives may know 8115 Vilakazi Street in Orlando West Extension as his address, given the number of raids they make there, hoping to catch him, but Liliesleaf is really now Nelson's home.

That first night, Wolfie spends it there with him. In the morning, construction workers arrive. Their job is to add more rooms to the original structure so that more people can stay here. Liliesleaf Farm was purchased so that it could be the *uMkhonto we Sizwe* base in Johannesburg.

Wolfie, who the construction workers know, introduces Nelson to them. 'Hello, everyone. This is David Motsamayi, and we have brought him here so that he can look after our property as you finish your work, to ensure no equipment is lost. He will also be responsible for cooking for you and do other odd jobs you require of him.'

His white liberal friends often like talking about the egalitarian nature of African societies: the dignity that Africans give each other when they speak in idioms so as not to embarrass each other. Nelson has often smiled at this, knowing it not to be the absolute truth that his friends – because of guilt over their superior lives based on race – like to think it is. And here, in his first days at Liliesleaf Farm, this is proven. He wakes up to make the workers – all Africans – breakfast, and serves them morning and afternoon tea. During the time they are there, they send him on errands for cigarettes, for more nails or whatever it is they require. They refer to him, a man they see as inferior to them, as either "boy" or "waiter".

They seem to take some pleasure in humiliating him and putting him in his place.

One afternoon, he is serving them tea when one of the men continues talking after he has handed him his teacup. Nelson stands in front of him so that he can add sugar and milk to his tea, but the man continues talking, gesticulating with his free hand. Seconds pass. Then a minute. The clock ticks and two minutes pass while this man continues speaking. Nelson moves on with the tray so that the other workers can also get their tea. The man who has been speaking upbraids him sharply, 'Waiter, come back here. I didn't say you could leave.' Nelson returns with his head hanging low.

When the workers leave at sunset, he too drives away. He goes to meetings, organizing and coordinating missions, then returns in the middle of the night. Alone, he sleeps lightly, constantly fearing and investigating every sound he hears. Security is of the greatest importance so he keeps the lights off and the gate locked at all times because he knows someone who looks like him driving a car in Rivonia will attract needless attention.

He is lonely, but soon the movement arranges it such that other people come and join him and help him get cover. The only way that Nelson can continue to stay there is if he has a white family to 'work for'. So into the main house move artist and designer Arthur Goldreich, his wife Hazel and their sons Nicholas who is eleven, and five-year-old Paul.

Arthur's politics are unknown to the police, so he makes a great cover but he is, in fact, a member of the Congress for Democrats and one of the first members of MK.

Mandela moves to the cottage like the gardener that he is now believed to be. The final addition to the smallholding of Liliesleaf Farm is a farm manager. It would otherwise be difficult to convince anyone that on a farm there is a gardener and other casual workers who come daily, but no white man to supervise them.

Winnie and the children can now visit.

It's a relief.

Winnie brings him an air rifle from home which he and Arthur use for target practice.

Once, during target practice, everyone spots a parrot perched high on a tree. Hazel teases Nelson that she doesn't think he will be able to hit the bird despite his many sessions of practice.

Nelson looks closely at the sparrow, aims and fires.

The sparrow falls.

Nelson is about to turn to Hazel to brag when five-year-old Paul goes to him with tears streaming down his face. 'David, why did you kill that bird?' the child asks, holding onto his overalls. 'Its mother will be sad.'

Nelson's delight at having hit the bird turns to shame. He wonders whether he has become his enemies and has lost his ability to value life. If he wasn't living under a pseudonym, if he was not pretending to be a gardener to his comrade, if South Africa was free for all who live in it – black, brown or white – he imagines Liliesleaf Farm in Rivonia would have been the life he would have wanted.

He and his wife Winnie would leave the house every day. She would drive, and drop him at his law offices in the city, then proceed to do her social work in Soweto. Maybe all his children would live with them and attend nearby schools.

On the weekends maybe they would all work in the garden – growing tomatoes, spinach, onions, pumpkins, beetroot. They would invite friends over or they could be invited to visit friends and they would share meals and drinks.

But this country and its apartheid system is abnormal, he thinks. And abnormal nations nurture abnormal people. Maybe, in a more normal society, I would not have killed the bird for no reason other than to prove I am a good shot.

11

PRELUDE TO AN EXIT

When Winnie visits with the children, life almost feels normal. Almost. Initially the visits happen often, but they have become less frequent. The police need to find The Black Pimpernel and they have figured one way to do this is to follow his wife. She will lead them to him. Through some complicated manoeuvring with different MK members, she still manages to make it over, but not as often as she used to. Not as often as the two of them would like. But then again, if it were up to them, the country would be free and they would see each other daily.

When she does make it, she comes with his children. Usually his youngest two – their daughters – and Makgatho, his second son by his first wife.

Zenani and Zindzi are still too young to know that

their father is a wanted man. They interact openly with him, but perhaps it's a good thing that, to them, the only name they know him as is *tata*. Their father. At eleven, Makgatho is old enough and has been sworn to secrecy not to reveal his father's identity. He guards this with the solemnity of an eleven-year-old who fears the police as only a child who has grown up seeing the police harass his family can.

He and the older Goldreich son, Nicholas, have become fast friends. Nicholas may be white and Makgatho African, his father may be considered a gardener and Nicholas's father a baas, but they are just two eleven-year-old boys and they have the same interests in cars.

One day Winnie visits with the three children. Zenani is playing with Paul. Zindzi is walking back and forth between her parents and showing off the words that she knows. Nicholas and Makgatho are playing outside. She calls all the children, including Paul and Nicholas to eat.

When Winnie visits, she brings Nelson some home-cooked comforts.

Today, a Sunday, when a plate of seven colours is served in many traditional South African households, she has decided to add a Xhosa touch to the meal. Instead of rice, she has made umngqhusho. She has added some curry to the samp and beans meal to make umngqhusho. Nelson is pleasantly surprised.

'Hawu curried umngqhusho?' he asks.

'Yes, curried umngqhusho,' she says, looking at him and laughing.

He joins her in the laughter as he knows that they are both sharing a memory.

On their first date, he took her to an Indian restaurant where, without consulting her, he ordered curried stew for both of them. He could have punched himself when, after a few forkfuls, she started complaining that the meal was too hot and ordered plenty of water. Now here she is, clearly having now acquired a taste for curry, adding it to a traditional Xhosa dish.

With the starch, she has made a chicken stew. When she opens the container, there is a homey, smokey smell with the chicken flavour and it fills Nelson with nostalgia of being back in his home village in Qunu. There is also beetroot, spinach, pumpkin, chakalaka and coleslaw salad to complete the seven colours. It's a true Sunday.

After everyone has eaten, Nelson tells the children to go and play outside. He needs to talk to his wife.

'But, David, we are also tired. What are we going to do outside?' Nicholas says, sighing.

'Here, take the *Drum* magazine, and you two big boys can read through it,' Nelson says. It's one of the things that Winnie brought him but he won't read it yet. He will read it only after they have left. For now, he needs to talk to Winnie.

Nicholas and Makgatho leave, holding the *Drum* magazine. They sit under a tree while going through the magazine together.

'Look at my side. It has a big house,' Makgatho starts.

'And my side has a Volvo,' Nicholas responds.

They continue going through the magazine, playing an age-old game of taking ownership of the two different sides. Perhaps it's their own way of having things to aspire to?

And then...

'That's my father,' Makgatho says, pointing to a picture of a beardless Nelson before he went underground.

'Why are you lying? That's not your father,' Nicholas answers.

'He is. He is my father,' Makgatho says, with even more conviction, his eyes now getting watery now that Nicholas, whom he thought was his friend, just called him a liar.

'But he cannot be, Makgatho. It says here: "Nelson Mandela". Your father's name is David,' Nicholas asserts.

'Are you my friend?' Makgatho asks solemnly.

'Of course I am your friend. Why?'

'Because I want to tell you a secret,' Makgatho says.

'Secret? I like secrets. I promise I won't tell.'

'Pinky swear?' Makgatho asks.

They cross their pinkies. This will be a secret.

Makgatho is not sure why he does it. He knows he did not like the way Nicholas spoke to his father before they got the magazine. Calling him 'David' so casually, without any respect. Like he was talking to his servant. Nicholas needs to know that his father is an important man. Maybe that's why he tells him.

'That *is* my father. David is his name but it's not his *name* name. His *real* name is Nelson,' Makgatho says.

Nicholas doesn't believe it, but he saw how upset Makgatho got a few minutes ago. He won't say anything to make him angry again. 'OK,' he nods, pretending he believes him. 'Hey, let's go and play with the dogs,' and off they run.

Later, after the family has left, Hazel comes over and chats to Nelson. 'Nelson,' she starts, 'something happened earlier between Makgatho and Nicholas.'

'What did Makgatho do?' Nelson wonders. His son has generally been a well-behaved boy.

'It appears that he and Nick were paging through *Drum* magazine when they saw an old image of you.' Hazel tells him the drama that ensued and that Nicholas backed off. But how, afterwards, Nicholas came to her to ask whether David's real name is Nelson. 'I'm not sure whether it's something to worry about too much but I thought I should let you know and you'll know how to deal with it.'

This is what happens when you stay for too long in any one place, Nelson thinks to himself. As it was at Wolfie's, is now and maybe ever shall be. He considers leaving immediately, but he decides not to. There is a chance that young Nicholas will say something to some of his school friends about the man he has believed to be his gardener, but he believes he is still safe for a time. The children are on holiday, and by the time schools open, he will be gone. On the cards is his first trip outside the country of his birth to a conference in Addis Ababa, Ethiopia.

Nelson spends the night before his departure at some friends' house with Winnie. She has brought him a packed suitcase for the journey. In her time with him before he undertakes this journey to a place neither of them has ever been to, she remains a stoic partner in marriage as much as she is in the struggle. She knows that the journey he is taking has to be done.

After Winnie leaves, Nelson goes to Soweto with another vehicle. He has an appointment with Walter, Duma and Ahmed 'Kathy' Kathrada, who are supposed to give him credentials for his journey. He arrives on time, as does Kathy.

Walter and Duma do not.

Nelson waits and waits without luck.

What he does not know is that, as they were each about to leave their homes, the police raided their houses and arrested them. These are the third raids since the first sabotages.

After a long time of waiting, he and Kathrada make other arrangements. Nelson is not a superstitious man. But his friends' absence leaves him with a sense of foreboding. He is slightly relieved when he is able to organize alternative transport. As the car that he has arranged approaches, he shakes his head and shrugs his shoulders in an attempt to shake off the feeling of fear. The fear does not leave him. He looks left. He looks right. He faces the front but sees no one apart from the people who should be there. Kathy massages his shoulder as one would a boxer getting into the ring.

'Courage, comrade. It shall be well.'

Nelson looks at Kathy and hugs him. He gets in the car and gives him the thumbs-up movement salute.

CAPTURED

Bruno Mtolo – saboteur – is arrested at his house in April 1962. The police come for him one evening while he sits with his wife, drinking Scotch. It's an illegal drink for those who look like him – a black man – but he does not care. A liquor store owner he knows arranged a bottle for him. He needs it. He and his team have just successfully bombed an electricity supply which put the city of Durban in darkness for some hours.

Someone had seen them. Someone who knew him. And now on this April night when he should be having a peaceful evening in his home, a dozen policemen land at his home unannounced. A dozen. As though he is capable of fighting even four off. They really need to be given more work. They beat him up and words he finds hurtful and unpleasant are used. One even spits in his face. He is furious, but with his hands cuffed behind his back, he cannot do anything.

When he gets to the police station, they remove Bruno's handcuffs and place him in a cell all alone. The three-quarters of a bottle of whisky he has drunk is now out of his system.

He is taken into an office. Two men, one black and another white, are seated there. He knows them both. Not only does MK have photographs of them both on their files, but he is friends with the black man's cousin.

Sergeants Marwa and Vorster.

'Hello, Bruno,' Vorster starts. 'My name is Sergeant Vorster and this here is Sergeant Maxwell Marwa. I think you know why we are here. Why you were arrested.'

Bruno shakes his head and then says loudly, 'No.'

Vorster laughs a smile that doesn't reach his eyes. His blue eyes are cold as steel. 'Would you like some tea or would you prefer more whisky?' Vorster asks him.

Bruno knows this is going to be thirsty work. He really could use some whisky. And he has heard stories about what happens when one is captured. What if it's the last drink he ever drinks? He is about to say 'whisky', but then he sees Maxwell's almost imperceptible shake of the head.

'I did nothing. I want nothing from you,' he answers.

Vorster smirks. 'OK. Don't say I didn't offer. You will regret it.' He continues, 'Look. Just give us the information we need and we will let you go. It's not you we want. It's information on the man who leads your unit here in Durban. That Ronnie Kasrils guy.'

Bruno cannot believe what he has just heard. Do they truly believe that a white man – a man who has achieved very little – is the one in charge of operations, and not him? Have they decided that people who look like him are so unintelligent that they cannot be in charge of what has happened?

'I don't know who you are talking about,' he responds.

Maxwell comes in. 'Look, we know you know. Just tell us.'

'I don't know him.'

'We've been watching you. We have eyes everywhere.' And then the photographs come out. Him and Ronnie shaking hands in greeting. Him outside Ronnie's place. Ronnie kneeling and tying up a package while he talks to someone.

Wait. That was the package that they set off. These people were watching them even then? They must have somehow escaped their watchers though, because they were not arrested before the explosives went off.

Still Bruno says nothing.

'You know what, Max? We are wasting our time being nice to this guy. Let's go. Bruno, ask the men here to make a telephone call when you are ready to talk.' Vorster and Maxwell stand up.

As they leave, three men come in. Bruno's hands are cuffed, and even before Maxwell and Vorster have closed the door, it begins.

'We are going to play some games until you are ready to talk,' one of them says while splashing water on him.

'You won't need these clothes, Native,' another says, while cutting the clothes from his body.

Then the beating begins. Bruno's wet body makes the pain sharper. It's as though they are all boxers and he is the punchbag they are practising their punches on. He passes out.

The next time they take him outside. There is a car. His hands are handcuffed at the back and he wonders where they are taking him. But they do not take him anywhere. One opens the bonnet. They bring out jump leads. They put them on the car battery, then they put the leads on his stomach. Bruno does not know what happens next as he passes out. They pour water on him. He wakes. They put the jump leads on him again.

It happens over and over and over again until they are tired or feel that he is about to die. They walk him back to his cell. He is in a lot of pain. Alone in his cell, he cries. Why didn't they just kill him? He wishes he *could* die. This is too much.

They keep him in a dark cell with no light. Anytime he feels he is recovering, they come in and torture him again. They give him electric shocks. They cover his face with a cloth, pour water on him until he feels he is about to die, then remove the cloth just when he thinks he is dying. They call it 'waterboarding'.

It's the third or maybe the fourth time they are torturing Bruno. He does not even know what day it is. But he does know he can't take it any more.

'Telephone. I will talk. Please please please telephone,' he says, and he is crying.

He is crying for the betrayal he feels he is about to make. He is crying for the pain he feels now. He is crying because he had no idea how costly it would be to get freedom. He is crying because he thought he was a strong man and now he knows that he is no longer that. He is crying because whatever he says will delay freedom by another day.

Some hours, maybe a day later, Marwa and Vorster arrive. And Bruno talks. He tells them everything. He tells them about Ronnie. He tells them about Nelson, who is out of the country – they are surprised, as they did not know this. He even tells them about his wife's annoying habits.

Then they release him with a final warning. 'Go, and do what you were doing before, but remember that you work for us now. Tell us everything. We know where you live.'

It's a beautiful clear day in Durban when Bruno Mtolo leaves the police station. But all he sees is the ugliness of life. He came in strong; now he leaves broken.

13

The time comes in the life of any nation when there remains only two choices: submit or fight! **THAT TIME** has now come to **South Africa!**

A FLEETING FREEDOM

To those in the know about *uMkhonto we Sizwe*, Nelson Mandela is the commander-in-chief.

And yet, apart from a few sabotage missions, he himself has been more a politician than a soldier. An organizer, not a fighter.

This needs to change, he decides. Emperor Haile Selassie of Ethiopia has arranged for him to get military training in his country. Nelson is met by the Foreign Minister who takes him to the headquarters of the Ethiopian Riot Battalion, where he learns how to be a soldier.

The amateur boxer has work to do as he goes through a tough process under a former guerrilla fighter. Training daily is from 8:00 a.m. in the morning until 1:00 p.m. An hour's lunch break follows, then more training from 2:00 to 4:00 p.m. This is then followed by a lecture on military science by the assistant police commissioner, Colonel Tadesse.

Nelson learns how to use both an automatic rifle and a pistol and takes target practice with the rest of the battalion. He takes part in 'fatigue marches' where he is expected to walk a certain distance within a certain time with only a gun, bullets and water. It is a serious test of endurance and it becomes his favourite exercise, as much for the way it helps him understand the landscape, as for the exercise.

In the study sessions, Colonel Tadesse teaches Nelson the importance of creating a liberation army. 'Unlike a regular capitalist army, a liberation army is egalitarian,' he says one evening as they are having tea. 'You must eat what they eat, and eat with them instead of isolating yourself.'

A sergeant walks in and asks the Colonel whether he may have an idea where a certain lieutenant might be. The Colonel glares at him. 'Can't you see I am talking to an important person? Why are you interrupting me when I am eating? Get out!' Nelson is taken aback at Tadesse's rudeness.

The six-month military training is cut down to eight weeks when the movement sends a message for Nelson to return home. He may be commander-in-chief of MK, but he gets his power from the movement and must follow directives.

Besides, the struggle is escalating back home and they need the commander-in-chief on the ground.

It takes experiencing freedom to understand oppression, Nelson reflects to himself on the final morning that he wakes up in Ethiopia. This feeling of freedom had first come to him when he landed in Mbeya, Tanganyika, after leaving apartheid South Africa eight months earlier. A fully independent African country.

When Nelson flew into Tanganyika from Bechuanaland, he was with one of his comrades, Joe. They checked into the hotel they were booked into. While they awaited a Tanganyikan official, who they were meeting on the veranda of their hotel, for the first time they got a feeling for what could be their future – a non-racial South Africa. People of all races were conversing and sharing meals.

As they sat there, it turned out the man they had been waiting for had been there all along. The man walked over to the reception and asked, while pointing to Nelson and Joe, 'Madam, did a Mr Mwakangale enquire to be called when these two gentlemen arrived?'

'I am sorry, sir. He did, but I forgot,' the receptionist said, blushing a deep red. She had just realized she was talking to Mr Mwakangale himself.

'Please be careful, madam,' the official had admonished. 'These men are our guests and we would like them to receive proper attention.'

Joe and Nelson had looked at each other in shock then. They could not believe that their host had just reprimanded a white woman!

Since then, Nelson had felt this freedom in Ghana after reuniting with Oliver, who is now based in London. And he has understood, more than ever, the need to fight for it when meeting his brothers from Algeria, who were fighting against the French. Away from apartheid South Africa, he has known what it means for a man not to be judged by the colour of his skin but by the measure of his mind and character.

It has been beautiful and mind-boggling and yes, sometimes unsettling. The first time he got on a flight piloted by someone who looked like him, he panicked. Ethiopian Airways. Would this man be able to take them to their destination safely? he had asked himself. Then he had realized. A professional man though he was, a lawyer, living in apartheid South Africa had damaged him. He had started questioning the ability of his own people to do certain things because in his country, there were jobs that were reserved for white men. So he sat back and relaxed and the flight was as smooth as the landing.

He has learned to stop being defensive. To know that when his ideas are dismissed, it is not because of the colour of his skin but because he was not convincing enough. This is what it has been like to be an African in Africa. What it should be like in all of Africa still under settler colonialism or, as is the case with South Africa, apartheid. When he goes back home, he wants to feel the same freedom of Ethiopia and Ghana and Guinea-Conakry and Nigeria and every other free country he has been to. He wants the people of the Rhodesias, of Bechuanaland, of Mozambique, of Angola, to feel this freedom too. And if he and they cannot be allowed this freedom, he wants them to fight for it.

Just as he plans to fight for it when he gets back home.

In the months Nelson has been away from home, he has known what it's like to have no one harassing him to show his pass. He has enjoyed walking leisurely, without fear of breaking a curfew imposed on him just for the colour of his skin. He has walked with his head held high, not fearing that those who think themselves of a superior race may consider him cheeky.

He has not had to pretend to be a cook, a gardener or a chauffeur to access spaces. Being himself with his ideas and ideals has been enough. He has not feared being considered illegal in this part of his own land. Away from apartheid and Verwoerd, Nelson has heard the sounds of freedom. He has known what freedom feels, tastes, smells and looks like.

And now, eight weeks after he began his training in Ethiopia, he is ready to return home and fight for that freedom.

14

HOME AGAIN

On landing in Kanye, Bechuanaland, from Tanganyika, Nelson is met by a local magistrate and security man. They are both white.

His blood runs cold. He does not feel safe in Bechuanaland because the British protectorate is still controlled by white people. Although relatively safer than South Africa, political activists have sometimes been kidnapped by the apartheid police from here.

The magistrate walks towards him and asks him his name.

'David Motsamayi,' he answers. He is close to home. He is not taking any risks.

The magistrate insists. 'No, please tell me your real name.'

Again Nelson answers. 'I said, I am David Motsamayi.'

'I was instructed to pick up Nelson Mandela from here,' the magistrate says. 'If you insist you are David Motsamayi and not Nelson Mandela, I shall have to arrest you since you have no permit to enter the country.'

Nelson panics. Either way, he shall be arrested. He shrugs his shoulders resignedly and says, 'If you insist I'm Nelson Mandela and not David Motsamayi, I shall not argue with you.'

The magistrate smiles. 'We expected you yesterday. Welcome back.'

The magistrate drives him to Lobatse to the home of a supporter of the movement. During their trip, the magistrate informs him that the South African police are aware of his return. He suggests that Nelson leaves the next day.

To be a guerrilla fighter is to be constantly alert and wary.

When the magistrate leaves, Nelson decides to leave the home of the supporter and go back to South Africa that very evening. With him is theatre director and MK member, Cecil Williams. Nelson gets behind the wheel. He is back to being David Motsamayi, chauffeur to one of his soldiers.

Cecil briefs Nelson on the situation at home. Then, well-versed in doing these cross-border trips, he sets off as he knows all the back roads that will get them from Bechuanaland into South Africa. They reach Liliesleaf Farm at dawn.

There is not much time to rest.

There is a war to be fought.

The following night, Nelson has a secret meeting with Walter, Moses and others. Nelson gives them a brief overview of his trip. He tells them the concern from the rest of the continent about their commitment to non-racialism at the expense of African nationalism. It is his and Oliver's belief, he tells them, that the free countries in Africa believe that the Africans must be seen to lead on matters concerning Africans without consulting with their Communist comrades from other races.

The people in the meeting decide this is a serious issue that they cannot tackle alone. Nelson must go to Durban and brief Chief Luthuli – the President General of the ANC – and hear what he has to say.

One of those present has reservations. He thinks Nelson should send someone else as his going is too risky. 'You are our commander-in-chief, Nelson, and on the Most Wanted list. You cannot afford to be caught,' he says.

They decide to vote on the concern. The man who proposed that Nelson stay put is overruled.

The next night Nelson leaves for Natal, again in the company of Cecil, and again posing as his driver.

Nelson meets up with Chief Luthuli and briefs him.

'This is problematic, Nelson,' the Chief says

slowly. 'We should avoid allowing a few foreign politicians to dictate policy for the movement.'

Nelson highlights that he does not believe that the foreign politicians are dictating policy, rather that they are failing to understand the movement's position.

The Chief wants to think about it further and chew on it. He will communicate later. That evening, Nelson has one more meeting.

He meets up with the MK Regional Command for Natal. It is the first time he meets Bruno Mtolo. Like many who have met Bruno, Nelson finds Bruno intelligent and articulate. Here, as everywhere, Nelson briefs them on his trip on the African continent. After the meeting, Nelson goes to the home of a photojournalist friend who has thrown a party in his honour, a combination of a 'welcome-home' and 'farewell' party.

After the meeting Bruno goes to make a call on a two-way radio.

'They are leaving tomorrow afternoon. Over,' he reports.

The voice on the other side relays a message back. A question.

'He is with a white male. Cecil Williams. Over.'

As Bruno sees someone walking towards him, he switches off the radio and puts it inside his trousers. He feels terrible. These men have become a band of brothers. But in a very fundamental way he does not feel bad. All he joined this movement for was so that he could gain freedom. To be able to sit in a restaurant and walk the pavements and work where he can without being discriminated against.

But no freedom is worth what he went through when they arrested him. He would rather be free from beatings and waterboarding and electric shocks by the police.

And he will say whatever they want him to say.

Nelson and Cecil are unaware of all this as they dance, drink and chat with their comrades at the farewell party.

In the morning, they return to their roles of chauffeur and baas. Cecil takes the wheel as Nelson sits on the passenger side. They are both looking forward to returning to Johannesburg, and Nelson is eager to see his wife and children again after so many months away.

Sometime later on the long journey Nelson notices a car behind them. 'Did you see that Ford V-8 behind us?'

Cecil says, 'I saw it. It's been following us from Pietermaritzburg.'

A moment later the car, full of white men, goes past them.

'Maybe we are both just overly worried,' Cecil adds hopefully.

And then the car that has passed them signals them to stop.

WHAT
HAPPENED NEXT

FREE NELSON MANDELA!

THE END OF APARTHEID

The police flagged down Nelson and Cecil's car. As they approached, Nelson hid the pistol that he had received as a farewell gift from Colonel Tadesse under the car seat. Possession of it would have likely earned him a death sentence.

Both Nelson and Cecil were arrested. His diary led the police to Liliesleaf Farm, where his other comrades, including Walter, were arrested.

The trial of the ANC members for acts of sabotage, designed to overthrow the apartheid system of South Africa, was known as the Rivonia Trial, named after the suburb of Johannesburg where a number of ANC leaders were later arrested.

At Liliesleaf, there was enough incriminating evidence to give the Rivonia Trialists a death sentence. There was also a star witness for the state known as Mr X: Bruno Mtolo, who gave further incriminating evidence. Luckily, the world seemed to sympathize with the prisoners, so a possible death sentence was commuted to a life sentence for Nelson Mandela and others, including Walter Sisulu.

In 1966, Verwoerd was killed as he entered Parliament. Dmitry Tsafendas, a parliamentary messenger and lifelong political militant, stabbed him. John Vorster took over as the Prime Minister. During his tenure as Prime Minister, Vorster oversaw the death and imprisonment of many children who protested at being forced to have classes in Afrikaans in 1976. He resigned as Prime Minister in 1978 and was succeeded by an even greater hardliner, P.W. Botha. During Botha's tenure as Prime Minister, many Africans in South Africa and neighbouring countries were killed by the police.

The world campaigned strongly for the end of apartheid, including banning South Africa's participation in international sports, carrying out 'Free Mandela' campaigns worldwide and applying economic sanctions. The campaigns were most intense in the 1980s.

Within South Africa, Winnie Mandela was at the forefront of those campaigns. She was arrested many times, and in 1977 she and a young Zindzi were banished to Brandfort, a township surrounded by farms, to a house which had no running water or electricity.

South Africa's neighbours, known as the Frontline States, were at the forefront of these campaigns by sheltering South African exiles, banning South African flights from using their airspace and refusing to trade with apartheid South Africa. South Africa retaliated by causing disturbances in neighbouring countries, and assassinating many activists and supporters. Among those who were killed were Ruth First, killed by a parcel bomb in Mozambique, and the Mozambican President, Samora Machel. There were also bombings by apartheid agents in Zimbabwe, Bechuanaland, Zambia and Angola.

In 1989, with the South African economy in shambles because of the economic sanctions and much fighting against the apartheid regime, P.W. Botha resigned after suffering a stroke.

F.W. de Klerk took over from him in August 1989. Considered a reformist, less than two months after he took office, de Klerk released Walter Sisulu and Ahmed Kathrada from prison.

On 11th February 1990, holding Winnie's hand, Nelson Mandela was released. He had spent twenty-seven years in prison.

In 1994, South Africans of all races voted in the first democratic elections and Nelson Mandela became the first President of a democratic South Africa.

TIMELINE

1912   A resistance movement is founded to protest against – among other things – the Natives Land Act, passed in 1913, which took lands from many of the native Africans and placed them in white hands.

1923   The resistance movement is renamed the African National Congress.

1944   The ANC Youth League is formed with younger people like Walter Sisulu and Oliver Tambo committed to creating non-violent mass action against injustice.

1946   The ANC forms an alliance with the South African Communist Party, working together to form a South African Mine Workers' Union. When the miners go on strike and it becomes a general strike, police brutality follows.

1948   The National Party, a right-wing and racist organization, wins the general election in South Africa. They start implementing the policy of apartheid.

1955   ANC, Indian, Coloured and white organizations meet in Kliptown and adopt the Freedom Charter, which demands equal rights for all whatever their race. This coalition refers to itself as 'the movement'.

1956	In December, 156 people, including Nelson Mandela, are arrested and take part in the longest trial in South African history – the Treason Trial. It lasts until 1961.
1959	Some of the younger members of the ANC break away and form the Pan-Africanist Congress (PAC).
1960	Members of the PAC, opposing a law that asks black people to carry passes in town, go to police stations and burn their passes. Police shoot and kill some of the protestors. In Sharpeville, not too far away from Johannesburg, 69 people are killed and 189 people are injured: the Sharpeville Massacre. The ANC and PAC are banned by the apartheid government.
1961	The last of the Treason Trialists are acquitted. Nelson Mandela goes underground. *uMkhonto we Sizwe*, the movement's armed wing, is formed with Mandela as its commander-in-chief.
1962	Nelson Mandela is captured and arrested.
1964	Mandela and some of his comrades are sentenced to life in prison after being convicted at the Rivonia Trial of sabotage.
1966	Prime Minister Verwoerd is killed as he enters Parliament.

Late 60s	African university students including Bantu Steve Biko form the Black Consciousness Movement (BCM).
1972–1973	The BCM helps to organize protests and workers' strikes. The apartheid government states that black development is treasonous.
1976	On 16th June, children all over the country march against the enforced teaching of Afrikaans in schools. In Soweto, the police shoot at students. Numbers of those killed during the Soweto Uprisings vary from 176 to 700.
1977	Winnie Mandela is forced to move to Brandfort with her daughter Zindzi.
1983	The apartheid government, under P.W. Botha, writes a new Constitution which co-opts Indians and Coloureds into Parliament to represent their racial groups. Africans are still not allowed. They call it the Tricameral Parliament.
1985	On 10th February at a rally in Soweto, twenty-five-year-old Zindzi Mandela reads out a speech from her father, rejecting a conditional offer of release by P. W. Botha which would mean the ANC would remain banned in return for his freedom. This famous speech is titled 'My Father's Speech'.

1986	On 19th May, apartheid agents set off simultaneous air and ground strikes in Botswana, Zimbabwe and Zambia.
1989	P.W. Botha resigns. F.W. de Klerk becomes the new President. He releases Walter Sisulu, Ahmed Kathrada and others.
1990	de Klerk un-bans the ANC, the PAC and other revolutionary movements. Nine days later, Mandela is released.
1994	Mandela becomes the first President of a fully democratic South Africa.
2021	Black South Africans still do not have land.

A LITTLE MORE ABOUT
NELSON MANDELA'S WORLD

AFRICAN NATIONAL CONGRESS (ANC)

Formed in 1912 to defend black South Africans'
rights and freedoms. After 1948, it also led the fight
against apartheid. It was banned in 1960 and its
leaders exiled or imprisoned, but in 1994, in the first
free elections in South Africa, it became the ruling
party, with Nelson Mandela as President. It has
remained in power ever since.

AFRIKAANS

A language spoken in South Africa, which derives
from the language spoken by Dutch settlers from
the seventeenth century onwards. Mainly spoken by
Afrikaners – descendants of those settlers. During
apartheid it was one of the two official languages (the
other being English), while African languages were
devalued. It is still spoken in South Africa, by about
14% of the population.

AMASI

Thick fermented milk, tasting a little like natural yoghurt. It is traditionally popular with black South Africans, but hardly ever drunk by whites.

APARTHEID

A policy of racial segregation adopted as law by South Africa's ruling National Party after the 1948 elections. It gave the highest status to the minority white population, lower status to the Asian and Coloured population, and the lowest status to black South Africans, who formed the majority of the population. Black South Africans could not attend the same schools as white children, or travel on the same buses. They could not marry white South Africans. They could not have the same jobs as whites, or live in white neighbourhoods. They could not vote in ordinary elections. Black political parties were banned. These laws remained until the early 1990s, and the effect of them persists today.

COLOUREDS

The name given to South Africans whose ancestry is a mixture of some of the different ethnic groups living in the country, for instance Koisan, Bantu, Afrikaans, White or Asian.

FREEDOM CHARTER

In 1955 the ANC asked thousands of people in the black townships and villages what freedoms they would like, and gathered them together in one long document – the Freedom Charter – which they officially adopted on 26th June 1955 at a meeting in Soweto.

NDOD'EMNYAMA WE VERWOERD
(WATCH OUT, VERWOERD)

This classic protest song was written in the 1950s by Vuyisile Mini, a member of the ANC. It carries a warning to the then-Prime Minister (and architect of apartheid) Hendrik Verwoerd, with the words (in the African language of Xhosa): 'Here is the black man, Verwoerd! Watch out, here is the black man, Verwoerd!' It was often sung at rallies.

THE SHARPEVILLE MASSACRE

On 21st March 1960 the police opened fire on a crowd of protestors who had gathered outside the police station in the township of Sharpeville, killing 69 and injuring 180 others, many of whom were shot in the back as they fled. Photographs of the scene led to widespread demonstrations. The National Party responded by declaring a state of emergency and detaining over 18,000 people. The ANC were banned and the MK formed shortly afterwards.

THE TREASON TRIAL

On 5th December 1956, the police arrested 156 people under the Suppression of Communism Act and put them on trial, accused of attempting to overthrow the National Party and replace it with a Communist government. The trial continued until 29th March 1961, when the final defendants were found not guilty and released.

UMKHONTO WE SIZWE OR 'MK' (SPEAR OF THE NATION)

The ANC's armed wing, formed with Mandela as its commander-in-chief, in 1961, a year after the Sharpeville Massacre. MK targeted police stations and governmental offices, but also places where civilians gathered, such as bars. They also mined roads. These actions inevitably led to civilian deaths. Particularly controversial was the 'Durban bombing' in 1986, when a beachside bar was blown up, killing three people.

UMNGQHUSHO

A traditional Xhosa dish of samp (corn kernels) and beans – Nelson Mandela's favourite meal.

XHOSA

After the Zulus, the Xhosa are the most populous indigenous people in South Africa, an ethnic group speaking their own language and living mainly in the Eastern Cape, in the south-east of the country. Nelson Mandela spoke Xhosa, and his grandson, Mandla, is now a Xhosa Chief.

ZULU

The largest ethnic group in South Africa, living mainly in the Natal region in the north-east of the country. This is the historic site of the Zulu kingdom as it existed when the British arrived in South Africa.

GLOSSARY

A-ge	Yes
Amandla	Power
Amaqhawe eNkululeko	Heroes of Freedom (Nguni)
Askies	Sorry/ Excuse (Afrikaans)
Awethu	Belongs to us
Baas	Boss (Afrikaans)
Dumelang	Hello (Sesotho)
Hambakahle	Go well
Hawu	An expression of surprise/ shock/confusion.
Molo	Hello (singular)
Molweni	Hello (isiXhosa plural)
Oom	Uncle (Afrikaans)
S'thandwa sam'	My love
Sawubona	Hello (isiZulu)
Sinjalo thina maZulu	We are like that, we Zulus
Skelems	Criminals
Tata	Father (familial term used by Mandela's children)
uMkhonto we Sizwe	Spear of the Nation (Nguni)
Vele	Well
Voetsek	Go away
Wena ke	You also/you too (Nguni, isiZulu, isiXhosa, Siswati)
Yebo	Yes

AUTHOR'S NOTE

Special thank you to:

The Nelson Mandela Foundation for providing access to Nelson Rolihlahla Mandela's travel diaries; author, MK veteran and former ambassador Ms Lindiwe Mabuza and Sisulu biographer, Elinor Sisulu, who both gave some clarity on certain historical aspects. Equally important, many thanks to Thula Simpson, whose book *UMkhonto we Sizwe: The ANC's Armed Struggle* was useful source material on the formation and early days of MK.

CALLING ALL TEACHERS AND EDUCATORS!

FREE ADDITIONAL RESOURCES AND MATERIALS FOR
TRUE ADVENTURES CAN BE DOWNLOADED FROM

www.pushkinpress.com/true-adventures

TRUE
ADVENTURES

INCREDIBLE PEOPLE
DOING INCREDIBLE THINGS

The most thrilling stories in history